William Henry Shelton

The Last Three Soldiers

William Henry Shelton
The Last Three Soldiers
ISBN/EAN: 9783337135997

Printed in Europe, USA, Canada, Australia, Japan

Cover: Foto ©ninafisch / pixelio.de

More available books at **www.hansebooks.com**

THE
LAST THREE SOLDIERS

BY
WILLIAM HENRY SHELTON

NEW YORK
THE CENTURY CO.
1897

WITH AN APOLOGY TO THE LITTLE SISTER
THAT THE PLOT IS NOT MORE BLOOD-CURDLING AND
HARROWING, THIS STORY OF WHAT MIGHT HAVE BEEN
IS AFFECTIONATELY DEDICATED TO HIS YOUNG
FRIENDS GUSSIE AND GENIE DEMAREST
BY THE AUTHOR

145 WEST FIFTY-FIFTH STREET,
NEW YORK, September 4, 1897

CONTENTS

Chapter		Page
I	Completing the Line	1
II	The Old Man of the Mountain	10
III	The Mountain of the Twentieth Red Pin	19
IV	A Day of Discoveries	23
V	The Cipher Code	36
VI	Messages of Dire Disasters	43
VII	In which the Three Soldiers Make a Remarkable Resolution	51
VIII	Which Ends in a Battle	62
IX	The Plateau Receives a Name	80
X	The Prisoners	93
XI	In which the Soldiers Make a Map	104
XII	How the Bear Disgraced Himself	121
XIII	How the Bear Distinguished Himself	136
XIV	Which Gives a Nearer View of the Neighbor called "Shifless"	152
XV	The Golden Mill	162
XVI	Which Shows that a Mishap is Not Always a Misfortune	178
XVII	How the Postmaster Saw a Ghost	190
XVIII	Knowledge from Above	201

CONTENTS

Chapter		Page
XIX	The Cave of the Bats	216
XX	The Stained-glass Windows and the Prismatic Fowls	232
XXI	A Scrap of Paper	243
XXII	The Deserted House	265
XXIII	Starvation	282
XXIV	The Rescue	298
XXV	Conclusion	315

LIST OF ILLUSTRATIONS

"'There They Are! See? By the End of the House!' Exclaimed Philip" . . . . . *Frontispiece*

                                                                                 PAGE

"It was a Mighty Fortress, Unscalable on its Western Side" 5

Andy Tells the Story of the Old Man of the Mountain 15

"Lieutenant Coleman was the First to Ascend, with the Telescope of the Station Strapped on his Shoulders" 25

"Corporal Bromley Took Position with a Red Flag having a Large White Square in the Center" . . 37

"Poor Philip, Left Alone, Burst into Tears" . . 53

The Mother Bear Comes for her Cub 69

"She Rose Suddenly on her Hind Feet and Dealt Him such a Whack as Nearly Broke his Ribs" . . 75

Christening the Territory 87

"The Fowls Hung about the Door" 107

"Philip Made Up the Most Marvelous Stories, which were Recited before the Fire" 115

"The Cask was Overturned so that the Yellow Pieces Poured Out upon the Floor" 131

"They Drove Him Off with Sticks and Stones" . . 143

LIST OF ILLUSTRATIONS

	PAGE
Making a Hundred-dollar Caster	149
The Golden Mill	165
Philip on the Edge of the Precipice	175
"Philip could See the Hole in the Snow through which He Knew He must have Fallen"	183
"Rushing Out from under the Trees, They Saw a Huge Balloon Sweeping over their Heads"	207
"Beyond the Illumination of his Torch He Saw Two Gleaming Eyes"	221
Exploring the Cave of the Bats	227
"He was Down on his Hands and Knees upon the Turf"	247
"The Scrap of Paper"	257
The Deserted House	269
The Grave of the Old Man of the Mountain	277
The Beacon Fire	291
"He could Only Cry Out, 'Fred! Fred! Here They Come!'"	303
"They Looked Hardly Less Comical than Before"	317

THE LAST THREE SOLDIERS

THE LAST THREE SOLDIERS

CHAPTER I

COMPLETING THE LINE

IF Andy Zachary, the guide, had not mysteriously disappeared from his home within the month which followed the events of the night of the 2d of July in the year 1864, sooner or later the postmaster in the Cove on one side and the people in the valley on the other must have learned of the presence of the little colony on the summit of the great rock.

On that particular night the cavalcade had come silently and secretly over the mountains by an unfrequented trail from the last station on Upper Bald, which towered above the Sandy River country. The troopers had followed the guide in single file along the ridges and down the stony trails, and now, when they emerged on the open Cove road for the first time, Andy fell back to the captain's side, in his butternut suit and mangy fur cap, with his long rifle slung behind his broad, square shoulders.

For that night his will was law above that of the captain; and before the three pack-mules at the end of the train had come out on the road, the head of the column had turned up a washout to the left, which presently brought the whole outfit into the shelter of a grove of pines alongside a deserted log cabin. It was just a trifle past midnight by the captain's watch, and the full moon which hung above the ridge to the west would light the Cove face of old Whiteside for yet an hour; and during the darkness which must follow in the small hours of the morning there would be ample time to steal through the sleeping settlement and find a lodgment high up on the mountain which was the objective of the expedition.

The troopers dismounted, and some lay down on the ground by the horses, while two kindled a fire in the stone chimney of the cabin and made coffee for the others. Corporal Bromley leaned a bundle of red-and-white flags against the door-post, and after turning aside with Lieutenant Coleman and Philip Welton to inspect their supplies on the pack-mules, the three joined the captain and the guide in the shadow of that end of the cabin which looked toward the singular mountain standing boldly between the Cove and the valley beyond. That it was a mighty fortress, unscalable on its western side, could be seen at a glance. The broad moonlight fell full on a huge boulder, whose mighty top, a thousand feet above the Cove, was fringed with a tall forest growth that looked in the distance like stunted berry-bushes, and whose rounded granite side was streaked with black storm-stains where the rains of centuries had coursed down. The moonlight picked out white spots underneath the huge folds which here and there belted the rock and protected its under face from the storms. These were the spots which the rills dribbled over and the torrents jumped clear of to meet their old tracks on the bulging rock below. It looked for all the world as if the smoke from huge fires had been curling against the mountain for ages, so black were the broad upward streaks and so white in the moon's light were the surrounding faces of the rock. Phil was the first to speak.

"It must have been a giant that rolled it there," he said with a sigh of relief, and looking up at Andy, the guide.

"Well, now, youngster," said Andy, "you 'd 'low so if you was round these parts in the springtime, when the sun loosens the big icicles hangin' on them black ledges, an' leaves 'em fall thunderin' into the Cove bottom."

The Cove post-office, whose long white roof crowned a knoll nearly in the center of a small tract within the mountain walls, Andy said, was at such times a great resort of the mountaineers, who came that they might watch the movement of the avalanches of snow and ice.

Because of its wonderful formation this mountain was of abundant interest to all during their brief halt, but it was examined most carefully by the three young soldiers who were to be stationed on its crest. Philip Welton was the youngest of the three, only just past seventeen, and it was well known to his officers that if he had not been an orphan, without parents to object, he would never have been permitted to enlist even as a drummer-boy in the 2d

Ohio, or in any capacity in any other command. The lad was of a gentle, affectionate nature, sensitive and refined, but his opportunities for education had been limited to the winter schools and the books he had read behind the flour-sacks in his uncle's mill. Some said his uncle was glad to be rid of him when he went away to the war. Like his friend and protector, Bromley, he had served with the colors on many a hard-fought field, and now the two had just been detached from their regiment and assigned to duty under the command of Frederick Henry Coleman, a second lieutenant whose regiment was the 12th United States Cavalry.

George Bromley, although the oldest of the three, was not yet twenty at the time he had enlisted at the beginning of the war, and he had left college in his junior year to enter the army.

Lieutenant Coleman had graduated from West Point the summer before, the very youngest member of his class. Although the three were mere boys at the time of their enlistment, each had entered the service through the strongest motives of patriotism, and each followed the fortunes of the national arms with an interest which showed itself in accordance with his personal character.

At that time General Sherman's army was engaged in that series of battles which began at Marietta, Georgia, and, including the capture of Pine and Lost Mountains, was soon to end in the victory at Kenesaw. The army of General Sherman was steadily advancing its lines in spite of the most heroic resistance of General Johnston, and

"IT WAS A MIGHTY FORTRESS, UNSCALABLE ON ITS WESTERN SIDE."

every new position gained was fortified by lines of log breastworks, sometimes thrown up in an hour after the regiments had stacked arms. These hastily constructed works, extending ten and twelve miles across the thickly wooded country, were nowhere less than four feet high, with an opening under the top log for musketry, and out in front the tree-tops were thrown into a tangled mass, almost impossible for an attacking army to pass. These peculiar and original tactics of General Sherman enabled him to hold his front with a thin line of men, while the bulk of his troops were sent around one flank or the other to turn the enemy out of his works and so gain a new position.

This was the sort of service Corporal Bromley and Philip Welton had been engaged in during the early part of the campaign; and when they remembered the long rains and the deep mud through which the soldiers marched, and the wagon-trains foundered and stuck fast, they were not sorry to be mounted on good horses and riding over hard roads.

Now that the moon had set, the troopers mounted again and moved quietly along the stony road, Andy Zachary, the guide, riding with the captain at the head of the column. The deep silence of the forest was on every hand, broken only by the clicking of iron shoes and the occasional foaming and plunging of a mountain stream down some laurel-choked gorge. The road wound and turned about, fording branches, mounting hills, and dipping down into hollows for an hour, until open fields began to appear

1*

bristling with girdled trees, and then the wooded side of the huge granite mountain shot up, towering over the left of the column. Soon thereafter the forest gave way to open country, and as the road swept round the base of the mountain it became a broad and sandy highway, so that when the horses trotted out there was only a light jangling of equipments,—sabers clicking on spurred heels, and the jingling of steel bits,—and when the pace was checked to a walk in passing some dark cabin only the creaking of the saddles was heard.

So it was that the troopers stole silently through the valley of Cashiers, with the solemn mountain-peaks standing like blind sentinels above the sparse settlement. Occasionally a drowsy house-dog roused himself to bark, and his fellow gave back an answering echo across the bushy fields; but no one of the sleepers awoke under the patchwork quilts of many colors, and the long rifles hung undisturbed over the cabin doors. Then the troopers exulted in their cleverness, and laughed softly in their beards, while the night winds blew over the roofs of the dark cabins as they passed.

After they were clear of the sandy road in the settlement, it was a long way up the mountain-side, and the iron shoes of the scrambling horses clicked on many a rolling stone, and some sleepy heads caught forty winks as they climbed and climbed. The cabins disappeared, and the fences, and the plow-steers in the hill pastures rattled their copper bells from below as the troop got higher; and so it was lonesome enough on the shaggy mountain, and every trace of the habitation of man had disappeared long before they reached the rickety old bridge which spanned the deep gorge.

Andy said that this bridge was the only possible way by which the top of the mountain could be reached, and that it had been built a great many years ago by a crazy old man who once lived on the mountain, but who was long since dead. It was still too dark to examine its condition. It could be seen that the near-by poles of the old railing had rotted away and fallen into the black chasm below. More than half of the bridge was swallowed up in the shadows of the foliage on the other bank. Away down in the throat of the gorge, where tall forest-trees grew and stretched their topmost limbs in vain to reach the level of the grass and flowers on the fields above them, a tinkling stream fell over the rocks with a far-away sound like the chinking of silver coins in a vault. The silence above and the murmur of the water below in the thick darkness were enough to make the stoutest hearts quail at the thought of crossing over by the best of bridges, so the captain prudently decided to wait for daylight; and as the distance they had gained above the settlement made the spot a safe encampment for a day, he ordered the troopers to unsaddle.

After feeding the tired horses from the sacks of oats carried in front of the saddles, the men lay down on the ground and were soon sleeping soundly under the tall pines which grew above the bridge-head.

CHAPTER II

THE OLD MAN OF THE MOUNTAIN

THE captain and Andy lingered by the bridge-head, and the three boy-soldiers who were to be left behind next day, long as the march had been, felt no inclination for sleep. They were too much interested in watching for the first light by which they could examine this important approach to their temporary station.

"I should like to know something more of the crazy old man who built this crazy old bridge," said Philip, appealing to Lieutenant Coleman. "Why not ask the guide to tell us?"

Andy was by no means loath to tell the story so far as he knew it, which was plain enough to be seen by the deliberate way in which he seated himself on a rock. Andy's audience reclined about him on the dry pine-needles.

Mountaineers are not given to wasting their words, and by the extreme deliberation of the guide's preparations it was sufficiently evident that something important was coming.

"Thirty years back," said Andy, taking off his coonskin cap, and looking into it as if he read there the beginning of his story, "and for that matter down to five year ago, there was a man by the name of Jo-siah Woodring lived all by himself in a log cabin about half-way up this mountain, and just out o' sight of the trail we-all come up tonight. He owned right smart of timber-land and clearin', and made a crap o' corn every year, besides raisin' 'taters and cabbage and onions in his garden patch. He had a copper still hid away somewhere among the rocks, where he turned his corn crap into whisky; and when Jo-siah needed anything in the line of store goods he hooked up his steer and went off, sometimes to Walhalla and sometimes clean up to Asheville.

"Now about a year after Jo-siah settled on his clearin', about the time he might have been twenty or thereabouts, when he come back from one of those same merchandisin' trips, instid of one steer he had a yoke, and along with him there was a little man a good thirty year older 'n Jo-siah, an' him walkin' a considerable piece behind the cart when they come through the settlement, same as if the two wa' n't travelin' together. The stranger was a dark-complected man, so the old folks say, and went just a trifle lame as he walked; and as for his clothes, he was a heap smarter dressed than the mountain folks. Not that he looked to care for his dress, for he did n't, not he; but through the dust of the road, which was white on him, hit was plain that he wore the best of store cloth.

" As the cart was plumb empty, hit would seem that the

little man fetched nothing along with him besides the clothes on his back, and such other toggery as he may have stowed away in the cowskin knapsack they do say he staggered under. If he had any treasure, he must 'a' toted hit in his big pockets, which, hit is claimed by some folks now livin', was stuffed out like warts on an apple-tree, and made him look as misshapen as he was small.

"Now, whether anybody heard the chinkin' o' gold or not (which I 'm bettin' free they did n't), hit looked bad for Jo-siah that this partic'lar stranger should disappear in his company, for he was never seen ag'in in the settlement, or anywhere else, by any human for a good two year after the night he come trudgin' along behind the cart. Hit was nat'ral enough that the neighbor folks in time began to suspicion that Jo-siah had murdered the man for his money, and all the more when he made bold to show some foreign-lookin' gold pieces of which nobody knowed the vally.

"They say how feelin' run consid'ble high in the settlement that year, but hit was only surmisin' like, for there was no evidence that would hold water afore a jury of any crime havin' been committed; and hit all ended in the valley folks avoidin' Jo-siah like his other name was Cain —and that sort o' treatment 'peared to suit him mighty well. Leastways, he went on with his plowin' and sowin' and stillin' his crap, and whistled at the neglect of his neighbors, who never came to the clearin' any more, and in that very year he built this bridge, with or without the help of the other one.

"When the bridge was first seen, hit was stained by the weather, and moss had come to grow on the poles, and rotten leaves filled the chinks of the slab floor as if hit had never been new, and no one cared to ask any questions of Jo-siah, who kept his own counsel and seemed to live more alone than ever. The bridge was only another mystery connected with the life of this man that everybody shunned, and nobody suspicioned that hit had anything to do with the disappearance of the other one, who was counted for dead.

"Now when day comes," said Andy, "you-all will see for yourselves that there is no timber on the other side o' this here gully tall enough to make string-pieces for a bridge of this length, and so the two string-pieces must have been cut on this side so as to fall across the chasm pretty much where they were wanted. Well, that was how it was; and the story goes that the man who first saw the bridge reported, judging by the stumps, that the right-hand timber had been cut six months or more before the other one, which might have been just about the time Jo-siah brought the stranger home with him, and would easily account for his disappearance onto the summit of the mountain, for of course you understand he was not dead, and Jo-siah the Silent had no stain of blood on his conscience.

"The mountain folks, however, thought different at that time, and looked cross-eyed at the painted cart drawed by the two slick critters on hits way to the low country. They was quick to take notice, too, when Jo-siah come back, that the cart carried more kegs than what hit had taken away, besides some mysterious-lookin' boxes and packages. Now this havin' continued endurin' several half-yearly trips, hit was the settled idee in the valley that Jo-siah was a-furnishin' of his cabin at a gait clear ahead of the insolence like of drivin' two steers to his cart when honest mountain folks could n't afford but one. Hit was suspicioned, moreover, that he was a-doin' this with the ill-got gold of the old man he had murdered, and the gals shrugged their shoulders as he passed, for no one of the gals as knew his goin's-on would set a foot in his cabin. It leaked out some way that Jo-siah had been investin' in books, which was the amazin' and crownin' extravagance of all, for hit was knowed that he could scarcely read a line of print or much more 'n write his own name.

"These unjust suspicions of murder and robbery against an innocent man continued to rankle in the minds of the valley folks for more than two years, until a most surprisin' event took place on the mountain, to the great disappointment and annoyance of those gossips who had been loudest in their charges against Jo-siah Woodring. Hit happened that two bear-hunters from the settlement found themselves belated in the neighborhood of this very bridge one September night, and, bein' worn out with the chase, they sat down to rest in the shadow of an old chestnut, where they soon fell asleep. They awoke just before midnight, and were about to start on down the mountain when they heard footsteps coming up the trail, and presently, dark as the night was, they saw a man with a keg on his

shoulder a-walkin' toward the bridge. The man was Jo-siah; and after restin' his burden on a stump and wipin' the sweat from his forehead, he shouldered hit again and tramped on over the bridge.

"The hunters were bold men and well armed, and, having had a good rest, they followed the man at a safe distance until he came to the ledge of rocks which you-all will view for yourselves by sun-up, and there he was met by a man with a ladder, who stood out on the rocks above. The hunters noticed that the stranger was a small man, and just then the moon came out from behind a cloud, and they knew him for the little old man who was supposed to have been murdered.

"When the hunters told what they 'd seen on the mountain, you may believe," said Andy, "there was right smart excitement in Cashiers, and some disappointment to find that Jo-siah was neither a murderer nor a robber. They went on hating him all the same for driving two steers to his cart and for having deceived them so long about the man on the mountain, and then they started the story that he was feedin' his prisoner on whisky, and that it was only a slow murder, after all. After that, one day, when Jo-siah had gone away to market, half a dozen of the valley men, with the two hunters to guide them, went up the mountain for the purpose of liberating that poor prisoner o' Jo-siah's.

"They carried a ladder along, and when they had climbed up the ledge they found a little log shelter not fit for a sheep-hovel; and as for the prisoner, he kept out of their way, for it was a pretty big place, with plenty of trees and rocks to hide among. Well, as the years went on, Jo-siah brought back less and less of suspicious packages in his cart when he came up from the low country; but it was known that he still went up the mountain on certain dark nights with a keg on his shoulder. The strange old man himself was seen at a distance from time to time, but at last his existence on the mountain came to be a settled fact, and the people ceased to worry about him.

"Well, five years ago, as I said," continued Andy, "Jo-siah took sick with a fever, and come down into the settlement to see the doctor; and he was that bad that the doctor had to go back with him to drive the cattle. He rallied after that so as to be about again, and even out at night; but three months from the time he took the fever he died. The doctor was with him at the time, and the night before he breathed his last he told the doctor that the little man on the mountain was dead. After the funeral another party went up to the top of the mountain, and, sure enough, there was the grave, just outside of the miserable shelter he had lived in so long; and it looks like he did, sure enough, drink himself to death, for there was no sign about the hovel that he ever cooked or ate ordinary food.

"The strangest thing about the whole strange business," said Andy, getting on to his feet, "is that there was nothing in Jo-siah's poor cabin worth carrying away; and if the old man did n't build this here bridge with his own hands thirty year ago, hit stands to reason that he helped Jo-siah."

CHAPTER III

THE MOUNTAIN OF THE TWENTIETH RED PIN

A FORTNIGHT before the events described in the opening chapter of this story, the topographical officer attached to General Sherman's headquarters might have been seen leaning over a table in his tent, busily engaged in sticking redheaded pins into a great map of the Cumberland and Blue Ridge Mountains. The pins made an irregular line, beginning at Chattanooga, and extending through Tennessee and North Carolina at no great distance from the Georgia border. Altogether there were just twenty of these pins, and each pin pierced the top of a mountain whose position and altitude were laid down on the map. After this officer, who was a lieutenant-colonel, had spent half the night, by the light of guttering candles, in arranging and rearranging his pins, he sent in the morning for the adjutant of a regiment of loyal mountaineers. Beginning with the first pin outside of Chattanooga, he requested the presence of a mountaineer who lived in the neighborhood of that particular peak. When the man reported, the colonel questioned him about the accessibility of the mountain under the first pin, its distance from that under the second pin, and whether each peak was plainly visible from the other. The colonel's questions, which were put to the soldier in the shade of the fly outside the tent where the map lay, brought out much useful information, and much more that was of no use whatever, because half the questions were intended to mislead the soldier and conceal the colonel's purpose. Sometimes he changed a pin after the soldier went away; and at the end of three days of interviewing and shifting the positions of his pins, the twentieth red head was firmly fixed above the point laid down on the map as Whiteside Mountain. Still a little farther along a blue-headed pin was set up, and then the work of the topographical officer of the rank of lieutenant-colonel was done.

These pins represented a chain of signal-stations, nineteen of which the captain of cavalry, with Andy Zachary to guide him, had now established one after the other, with as much secrecy as the lieutenant-colonel had employed in selecting the positions. And now the gray dawn was coming on the side of the twentieth mountain as Andy finished his story. In fact, as the last word fell from his lips a lusty cock tied on one of the pack-saddles set up a shrill crow to welcome the coming day. Although tall pines grew thick about the bridge-head where the troopers were still sleeping, it was light enough to see that only low bushes and gnarled chestnuts grew on the other bank. The noisy branch kept up its ceaseless churning and splashing among the rocks far down in the throat of the black gorge, and the great height and surprising length of its single span made the crazy old bridge look more treacherous than ever. It swayed and trembled with the weight of the captain by the time he had advanced three steps from the bank, so that he came back shaking his head in alarm. By this time the men were afoot, and Andy asked for an ax, which at the first stroke he buried to its head in the rotten string-piece.

"Just what I feared," said the captain. "Do you think I am going to trust my men on that rotten structure?"

Andy said nothing in reply as he kicked off with his boot a huge growth of toadstools, together with the bark and six inches of rotten wood from the opposite side of the log. Then he struck it again with the head of the ax such a blow that the old sticks of the railing and great sections of bark fell in a shower upon the tree-tops below. The guide saw only consternation in the faces of the men as he looked around, but there was a smile on his own.

"Hit may be old," said Andy, throwing down the ax, "but there is six inches of tough heart into that log, and I'd trust hit with a yoke o' cattle." With that he strode across to the other side, and coming back jounced his whole weight on the center, with only the effect of rattling another shower of bark and dry fungi into the gorge.

"Bring me one of the pack-mules," cried Andy; and presently, when the poor brute arrived at the head of the old causeway, it settled back on its stubborn legs and refused to advance. At this the guide tied a grain-sack over the animal's eyes and led him safely across. Lieutenant Coleman led over the second mule by the same device, and Bromley the third. By this time it was broad daylight, and the captain detailed three men to help in the unpacking. These he sent over one at a time, so that after himself Philip was the last to cross.

Beyond was an open field where blue and yellow flowers grew in the long, wiry grass, which was wet with the dew. This grass grew up through a thick mat of dead stalks, which was the withered growth of many years. Under the trees and bushes the leaves had rotted in the rain where they had fallen, or in the hollows where they had been tossed by the wandering winds. There was not a sign of a trail, nor a girdled tree, nor a trace of fire, nor any evidence that the foot of man had ever trodden there. The little party seemed to have come into an unknown country, and after crossing the open field they continued climbing up a gentle ascent, winding around rocks and scraggly old chestnut-trees, until they arrived under the ledge which supported the upper plateau. This was found to extend from the boulder face on the Cove side across to a mass of shelving rocks on the Cashiers valley front, and was from thirty to fifty feet in height, of a perpendicular and bulging fold in the smooth granite. After a short exploration a place was found where the ledge was broken by a shelf or platform twenty feet from the ground; and just here, in the leaves and grass below, lay the rotted fragments of a ladder which had doubtless been used by the old man of the mountain himself.

CHAPTER IV

A DAY OF DISCOVERIES

WHILE Andy, with the help of the detail, was cutting and notching the timber for ladders, the captain and the three young soldiers of the station made a breakfast, standing, from their haversacks and canteens, and looked about them over the wild country at their feet, and off at the blue peaks which rose above and around the valley of Cashiers, and then at the ridges in the opposite direction, drawn like huge furrows across the western horizon, showing fainter and fainter in color until the blue of the land was lost in the blue of the sky.

The men worked with a will, so that by ten o'clock the main ladder, which was just a chestnut stick deeply notched on the outer side, was firmly set in the ground against the face of the cliff. The landing-shelf was found to extend into a natural crevice, so that the short upper ladder was set to face the bridge, and so as to be entirely concealed from the view of any one approaching from below.

When everything was in readiness, Lieutenant Coleman was the first to ascend, with the powerful telescope of the station strapped on his shoulders; and the others quickly followed, except the three troopers who remained behind to unpack the mules and bring up the rations and outfit for the camp.

At the point where they landed there was little to be seen of the top of the mountain beyond a few stunted chestnuts which clung to the rocks and were dwarfed and twisted by the wind; and nearly as many dead blue limbs lay about in the thin grass as there were live green ones forked against the sky. There was the suggestion of a path bearing away to the left, and following this they came to a series of steps in the rocks, partly natural and partly artificial, which brought them on to a higher level where an extended plateau was spread out before them. On the western border they saw the line of trees overhanging the Cove side—the same that had looked like berry-bushes the night before from the cabin where they had halted for the moon to go down. From this point the crest of the Upper Bald was in plain view across the Cove, but, anxious as they were to open communication with the other mountain, the flags had not yet come up, and there was nothing left for them to do but continue their exploration. It was observed, however, that the trees overhanging the Cove would conceal the flagging operations from any one who might live on the slopes of the mountains in that direction, and, moreover, that by going a short distance along the ridge to the right a fine

"LIEUTENANT COLEMAN WAS THE FIRST TO ASCEND, WITH THE TELESCOPE OF THE STATION STRAPPED ON HIS SHOULDERS."

backing of dark trees would be behind the signal-men. Philip would have scampered off to explore and discover things for himself, but the captain restrained him and directed that the party should keep together. Andy carried his long rifle, and Philip and Bromley had brought up their carbines, so that they were prepared for any game they might meet, even though it were to dispute progress with a bear or panther. Since they had come up the ladders the region was all quite new to Andy, and he no longer pretended to guide them.

Back from the last ridge the ground sloped to a lower level, much of which was bare of trees and so protected from the wind that a rich soil had been made by the accumulation and decay of the leaves. At other points there were waving grass and clumps of trees, which latter shut off the view as they advanced, and opened up new vistas as they passed beyond them. It could be seen in the distance, however, that the southern end of the plateau was closed in by a ledge parallel to and not unlike that which they had already scaled, except that it was much more formidable in height.

There was a stream of clear, cold water that was found to come from a great bubbling spring. It broke out of the base of this southern ledge, and after flowing for some distance diagonally across the plateau tumbled over the rocks on the Cashiers valley side and disappeared among the trees.

After inspecting this new ledge, which was clearly an impassable barrier in that direction, and as effectually

2*

guarded the plateau on that side as the precipices which formed its other boundaries, the captain and his party turned back along the stream of water, for a plentiful supply of water was more to be prized than anything they could possibly discover on the mountain.

"There is one thing," said Andy, as they walked along the left bank of the stream, "that you-all can depend no. Risin' in the spring as hit does, that branch will flow on just the same, summer or winter."

"Probably," said Lieutenant Coleman; "but then, you know, we are not concerned about next winter."

A little farther on a rose-bush overhung the bank, and at the next turn they found a grape-vine trailing its green fruit across a rude trellis, which was clearly artificial. A few steps more and they came to a foot-log flattened on the top; and, although it tottered under them, they crossed to the other side, and coming around a clump of chinkapin-bushes, they found themselves at the door of a poor hut of logs, whose broken roof was open to the rain and sun. The neglected fireplace was choked with leaves, and weeds and bushes grew out of the cracks in the rotting floor; and, surely enough, in one dry corner stood the very brown keg that Josiah Woodring had brought up the mountain. In the midst of the dilapidation and the rotting wood about it, it was rather surprising that the cask should be as sound as if it were new, and the conclusion was that it had been preserved by what it originally contained.

Just then there was a cry from Philip, who had gone to

the rear of the hovel; and he was found by the others leaning over the grave of the old man of the mountain, and staring at the thick oak headboard, which bore on the side next the cabin these words:

ONE WHO WISHES TO BE FORGOTTEN.

The letters were incised deep in the hard wood, and seemed to have been cut with a pocket-knife. It was evident from the amount of patient labor expended on the letters that the work had been done by the unhappy old man himself, perhaps years before he died. Of course it had been set up by Josiah, who must have laid him in his last resting-place.

"That looks like Jo-siah was no liar, any more than he was a murderer and robber," said Andy; "and if the little man could live up here twenty-five years, I reckon you young fellers can get along two months."

A spot for camp was selected a few rods up the stream from the poor old cabin and grave. This was at a considerable distance from the ridge where the station was to be, but it had two advantages to balance that one inconvenience. In the first place, it was near the water, and then no smoke from the cook-fire would ever be seen in the valley below. Accordingly, the stores were ordered to be brought to this point, and Corporal Bromley hurried away to the head of the ladders to detain such articles as would be needed at the station on the ridge. Below the ledge the mules could be seen quietly browsing the grass, and, to the annoyance of Lieutenant Coleman, a blue haze was softly enveloping the distant mountains, as in a day in Indian summer, so that it was no longer possible to think of communicating with the next station, which was ten miles away.

That being the case, the afternoon was spent in pitching the tents and making the general arrangements of the camp. Owing to the difficulty of transportation, but the barest necessaries of camp life were provided by the government; and, notwithstanding his rank, Lieutenant Coleman had only an "A" tent, and Bromley and Philip two pieces of shelter-tent and two rubber ponchos. It was quickly decided by the two soldiers to use their pieces of tent to mend the roof of the hut of the old man of the mountain, and to store the rations as well as to make their own quarters therein. From the Commissary Department their supplies for sixty days consisted precisely of four 50-pound boxes of hard bread, 67 pounds 8 ounces bacon, 103 pounds salt beef, 27 pounds white beans, 27 pounds dry peas, 18 pounds rice, 12 pounds roasted and ground coffee, 8 ounces tea, 27 pounds light-brown sugar, 7 quarts vinegar, 21 pounds 4 ounces adamantine candles, 7 pounds 4 ounces bar soap, 6 pounds 12 ounces table-salt, and 8 ounces pepper. The medical chest consisted of 1 quart of commissary whisky and 4 ounces of quinine. Besides the flags and telescope for use on the station, their only tools were an ax and a hatchet. On ordinary stations it was the rule to furnish lumber for building platforms or towers, but here they were provided with only a coil of wire and ten pounds of nails, and if platforms were necessary to get above the surrounding trees they must rely upon such timber as they could get, and upon the ax to cut away obstructions. Fortunately for this particular station, they could occupy a commanding ridge and send their messages from the ground.

Philip had by some means secured a garrison flag, which was no part of the regular equipment; and through Andy they had come into possession of a dozen live chickens and a bag of corn to feed them. On the afternoon before the departure of the troopers, the captain, who had now established the last of the line of stations, confided to Lieutenant Coleman his final directions and cautions. He asked Andy to point out Chestnut Knob, which was the mountain of the blue pin, and whose bald top was in full view to the right of Rock Mountain, and not more than eight miles away in a southeasterly direction, and, as Andy said, just on the border of the low country in South Carolina. This was the mountain, the captain informed Lieutenant Coleman, from which in due time, if everything went well in regard to a certain military movement, he would receive important messages to flag back along the line.

What this movement was to be was still an official secret at headquarters, and Lieutenant Coleman would be informed by flag of the time when he would be required to be on the lookout for a communication from the mountain of the blue pin. At the close of his directions, the captain, standing very stiff on his heels and holding his cap in his hand, made a little speech to Lieutenant Coleman, in which he complimented him for his loyalty and patriotic devotion to the flag, and reminded him that in assigning him to the last station the commanding general had thereby shown that he reposed especial confidence in the courage, honor, and integrity of Lieutenant Frederick Henry Coleman of the 12th Cavalry, and in the intelligence and obedience of the young men who were associated with him. This speech, delivered just as the shadows were deepening on the lonely mountain-top, touched the hearts of the three boys who were so soon to be left alone, and was not a whit the less impressive because Andy plucked off his coonskin cap and cried, in his homely enthusiasm, that "them was his sentiments to the letter!"

It was understood that there should be no signaling by night, and no lights had been provided for that purpose; so that, there being nothing to detain them on the plateau, they decided to accompany the captain and Andy back to the bridge and see the last of the escort as it went down the mountain.

Two of the troopers, contrary to orders, had during the day been as far as the deserted cabin of Josiah Woodring, and one of these beckoned Philip aside and told him where he would find a sack of potatoes some one had hidden away on the other side of the gorge, which, with much disgust, he described as the only booty they had found worth bringing away.

So great is the love of adventure among the young that there was not one of the troopers but envied his three comrades who were to be left behind on the mountain; but it was a friendly rivalry, and, in view of the possibilities of wild game, they insisted upon leaving the half of their cartridges, which were gladly accepted by Philip and Bromley.

The moon was obscured by thick clouds, and an hour before midnight the horses were saddled, and with some serious, but more jocular, words of parting, the troopers started on the march down the mountain, most of them hampered by an additional animal to lead. The captain remained to press the hand of each of the three young soldiers, and when at last he rode away and they turned to cross the frail old bridge, whose unprotected sides could scarcely be distinguished in the darkness, they began to realize that they were indeed left to their own resources, and to feel a trifle lonely, as you may imagine.

Before leaving that side of the gorge, however, Corporal Bromley had shouldered their precious cartridges, which had been collected in a bag, and on the other side Philip secured the sack of potatoes; and thus laden they trudged away across the open field and among the rocks and bushes, guided by the occasional glimpses they had of the cliff fringed with trees against the leaden sky. It was of the first importance that the cartridges should be kept dry, and to that end they hurried along at a pace which scattered them among the rocks and left but little opportunity for conversation. Lieutenant Coleman was in advance, with Philip's carbine on his arm; next came Corporal Bromley, with the cartridges; and a hundred yards behind,

Philip was stumbling along with the sack of potatoes on his shoulder. They had advanced in this order until the head of the straggling column was scarcely more than a stone's throw from the cliff, when a small brown object, moving in the leaves about the foot of the ladder, uttered a low growl and then disappeared into the deeper shadow of the rock. At the same moment the rain began to fall, and Corporal Bromley stepped one side to throw his bag of cartridges into the open trunk of a hollow chestnut. While he was thus engaged, with the double purpose of freeing his hands and securing the cartridges from the possibility of getting wet, his carbine lying on the ground where he had hastily thrown it, Lieutenant Coleman fired at random at the point where he had indistinctly seen the moving object. The darkness had increased with the rain, and as the report of the carbine broke the quiet of the mountain a shadowy ball of fur scampered by him, scattering the leaves and gravel in its flight. The mysterious object passed close to Bromley as he was groping about for his weapon, and the next moment there was a cry from Philip, who had been thrown to the ground and his potatoes scattered over the hillside.

"Whatever it was," said Philip, when he presently came up laughing at his mishap, "I don't believe it eats potatoes, and I will gather them up in the morning."

As it was too dark for hunting, and the cartridges were in a safe place, Lieutenant Coleman and Corporal Bromley slung their carbines and followed Philip, who was the first to find the foot of the ladder.

It was not so dark but that they made their way safely to the camp, and, weary with the labors of the day, they were soon fast asleep in their blankets, unmindful of the rain which beat on the "A" tent and on the patched roof of the cabin of the old man of the mountain.

CHAPTER V

THE CIPHER CODE

ON the morning of July 4 the sun rose in a cloudless sky above the mountains, and the atmosphere was so clear that the most remote objects were unusually distinct. The conditions were so favorable for signaling that, after a hurried breakfast, the three soldiers hastened to the point on the ridge which they had selected for a station. Corporal Bromley took position with a red flag having a large white square in the center, and this he waved slowly from right to left, while Lieutenant Coleman adjusted his spy-glass, resting it upon a crotched limb which he had driven into the ground; and at his left Philip sat with a note-book and pencil in hand, ready to take down the letters as Lieutenant Coleman called them off. There are but three motions used in signaling. When the flag from an upright position is dipped to the right, it signifies 1; to the left, 2; and forward, 3. The last motion is used only to indicate that the end of the word is reached. Twenty-six combinations of the figures 1 and 2 stand for the letters of the alphabet.

"CORPORAL BROMLEY TOOK POSITION WITH A RED FLAG HAVING A LARGE WHITE SQUARE IN THE CENTER."

THE CIPHER CODE

It is not an easy task to learn to send messages by these combinations of the figures 1 and 2, and it is harder still to read the flags miles away through the telescope. The three soldiers had had much practice, however, and could read the funny wigwag motions like print. If any two boys care to learn the code, they can telegraph to each other from hill to hill, or from farm to farm, as well as George and Philip. You will see that the vowels and the letters most used are made with the fewest motions— as, one dip of the flag to the left (2) for I, and one to the right (1) for T. Z is four motions to the right (1111); and here is the alphabet as used in the signal-service:

A,	11,		O,	12,
B,	1221,		P,	2121,
C,	212,		Q,	2122,
D,	111,		R,	122,
E,	21,		S,	121,
F,	1112,		T,	1,
G,	1122,		U,	221,
H,	211,		V,	2111,
I,	2,		W,	2212,
J,	2211,		X,	1211,
K,	1212,		Y,	222,
L,	112,		Z,	1111,
M,	2112,		&,	2222,
N,	22,		ing,	1121,
		tion, 2221.		

When the flag stops at an upright position, it means the end of a letter—as, twice to the right and stop (11) means A; one dip forward (3) indicates the end of a word; 33, the end of a sentence; 333, the end of a message. Thus 11-11-11-3 means "All right; we understand over here; go ahead"; and 11-11-11-333 means "Stop signaling." Then 212-212-212-3 means "Repeat; we don't understand what you are signaling"; while 12-12-12-3 means "We have made an error, and if you will watch we will give the message to you correctly."

Now, if Lieutenant Coleman wanted to say to another signal-officer "Send one man," the sentence would read in figures, "121, 21, 22, 111, 3, 12, 22, 21, 3, 2112, 11, 22, 33." But in time of war the signalmen of the enemy could read such messages, and so each party makes a cipher code of its own, more or less difficult; and the code is often changed. So if Lieutenant Coleman's cipher code was simply to use for each letter sent the fourth letter later in the alphabet, his figures would have been quite different, and the letters they stood for would have read:

W-i-r-h s-r-i q-e-r.
S-e-n-d o-n-e m-a-n.

So, after fifteen minutes of waiting, during which time the flag in Corporal Bromley's hand made a great rustling and flapping in the wind, moving from side to side, Lieutenant Coleman got his glass on the other flag, ten miles away, and found it was waving 11-11-11-3—"All right." Corporal Bromley then sent back the same signal, and sat down on the bank to rest. What Lieutenant Coleman saw at that distance was a little patch of red dancing about on the object-glass of his telescope; he could not see even the man who waved it, or the trees behind him. Promptly at Bromley's signal "All right," the little object came to a rest; and when it presently began again, Lieutenant Coleman called off the letters, which Philip repeated as he entered them in the book. For an hour and a half the messages continued repeating all the mass of figures which had come over the line during the last three days.

When the mountain of the nineteenth red pin had said its say as any parrot might have done, for it was absolutely ignorant of the meaning of the figures it received and passed on (for the reason that it had no officer with the cipher), Lieutenant Coleman took from his pocket a slip of paper on which he had already arranged his return message to Chattanooga. When this had been despatched, the lieutenant took the note-book from Philip, and went away to his tent to cipher out the meaning of the still meaningless letters.

They were sufficiently eager to get the latest news, for they knew that the army they had just left had been advancing its works and fighting daily since the twenty-second day of June for the possession of Kenesaw Mountain. The despatches were translated in the order in which they came, so that it was a good half-hour before Lieutenant Coleman appeared with a radiant face to say that General Sherman had taken possession of Kenesaw Mountain on the day before. "And that is not all," he cried, holding up his hand to restrain any premature outburst of enthusiasm. "Listen to this! 'The "Alabama" was sunk by the United States steamer "Kearsarge" on the nineteenth day of June, three miles outside the harbor of Cherbourg, on the coast of France.'"

Corporal Bromley was not a demonstrative man, yet the blood rushed to his face, and there was a glittering light in his eyes which told how deeply the news touched him; but Philip, on the contrary, was wild with delight, and danced and cheered and turned somersaults on the grass.

CHAPTER VI

MESSAGES OF DIRE DISASTERS

"WHAT a pity," cried Philip, "that the boys on the next mountain should be left in ignorance of these victories when we could so easily send them the news without using the cipher—and this the Fourth of July, too!"

That form of communication, however, was strictly forbidden by the severe rules of the service, and it was the fate of Number 19 to remain in the dark, like all the other stations on the line, except the first and tenth and their own, which alone were in charge of commissioned officers who held the secret of the cipher.

The news of the destruction of the "Alabama," which had been the terror of the National merchant-vessels for two years, was of the highest importance, and would cause great rejoicing throughout the North. Although the battle with the "Kearsarge" had taken place on June 19, it must be borne in mind that this period was before the permanent laying of the Atlantic cable, and European news was seven and eight days in crossing the ocean by the foreign steamers, and might be three days late before it started for this side, in case of an event which had happened three days before the sailing of the steamer. After several unsuccessful attempts, a cable had been laid between Europe and America in 1858, three years before the beginning of the great war, and had broken a few weeks after some words of congratulation had passed between Queen Victoria and President Buchanan. Some people even believed that the messages had been invented by the cable company, and that telegraphic communication had never been established at all along the bed of the ocean. At all events, news came by steamer in war-times, and so it happened that these soldiers, who had been three days in the wilderness, heard with great joy on July 4 of the sinking of the "Alabama," which happened on the coast of France on June 19.

The garrison flag was raised on a pole over the "A" tent, and the day was given up to enjoyment, which ended in supping on a roast fowl, with such garnishings as their limited larder would furnish. On this occasion Lieutenant Coleman waived his rank so far as to preside at the head of the table,—which was a cracker-box,—and after the feast they walked together to the station and sat on the rocks in the moonlight to discuss the military situation.

If General Grant had met with some rebuffs in his recent operations against Petersburg in Virginia, he was steadily closing his iron grasp on that city and Richmond; and not one of these intensely patriotic young men for a moment doubted the final outcome. Philip and Lieutenant Coleman had been much depressed by the recent disaster, and the news of the morning greatly raised their spirits. If Bromley was less excitable than his companions, the impressions he received were more enduring; but, on the other hand, he would be slower to recover from a great disappointment.

"The reins are in a firm hand at last," said Lieutenant Coleman, referring to the control then recently assumed by General Grant, "and now everything is bound to go forward. With Grant and Sheridan at Richmond, Farragut thundering on the coast, the 'Alabama' at the bottom of the sea, and 'Uncle Billy forcing his lines nearer and nearer to Atlanta, we are making brave progress. I believe, boys, the end is in sight."

"Amen!" said Corporal Bromley.

"Hurrah!" cried Philip.

"You boys," continued Lieutenant Coleman, "have enlisted for three years, while I have been educated to the profession of arms; but if this rebellion is not soon put down I shall be ashamed of my profession and leave it for some more respectable calling."

So they continued to talk until late into the night, cheered by the good news they had heard, and very hopeful of the future.

The following day was foggy, and Philip went down the ladder to bring up the potatoes, which he had quite forgotten in the excitement of the day before. Bromley, too, paid a visit to the tree where he had thrown in the cartridges; but the opening where he had cast in the sack was so far from the ground that it would be necessary to use the ax to recover it, and as he could find no drier or safer storehouse for the extra ammunition, he was content to leave it there for the present. Lieutenant Coleman busied himself in writing up the station journal in a blank-book provided for that purpose.

When Philip found his potatoes, which had been scattered on the ground where he had been thrown down in the darkness by the mysterious little animal, he was at first disposed to leave them, for they were so old and shrunken and small that he began to think the troopers had been playing a joke on him. But when he looked again, and saw the small sprouts peeping out of the eyes, a new idea came to him, and he gathered them carefully up in the sack. He bethought himself of the rich earth in the warm hollow of the plateau, where the sun lay all day, and where vegetation was only smothered by the coating of dead leaves; and he saw the delightful possibility of having new potatoes, of his own raising, before they were relieved from duty on the mountain. What better amusement could they find in the long summer days, after the morning messages were exchanged on the station, than to cultivate a small garden? If he had had the seeds of flowers, he might have thrown away the wilted potatoes; but next to the cultivation of flowers came the fruits of the earth, and if his plantation never yielded anything, it would be a pleasure to watch the vines grow. Lieutenant Coleman readily gave his consent; and, after raking off the carpet of leaves with a forked stick, the soft, rich soil lay exposed to the sun, so deep and mellow that a piece of green wood, flattened at the end like a wedge, was sufficient to stir the earth and make it ready for planting. Philip cut the potatoes into small pieces, as he had seen the farmers do, and with the help of the others, who became quite interested in the work, the last piece was buried in the ground before sundown.

On the following morning the flags announced that, in a cavalry raid around Petersburg, General Wilson had destroyed sixty miles of railroad, and that forty days would be required to repair the damage done to the Danville and Richmond road. During the next three days there was no news worth recording, and the fever of gardening having taken possession of Philip, he planted some of the corn they had brought up for the chickens, and a row each of the peas and beans from their army rations.

The 10th of July was Sunday, the first since they had been left alone on the mountain; and Lieutenant Coleman required his subordinates to clean up about the camp, and at nine o'clock he put on his sword and inspected quarters like any company commander. After this ceremony, Philip read a psalm or two from his prayer-book, and Corporal Bromley turned over the pages of the Blue Book, which was the Revised Army Regulations of 1863. These two works constituted their limited library.

There was a dearth of news in the week that followed, and what little came was depressing to these enthusiastic young men, to whom the temporary inactivity of the army which they had just left was insupportable.

On Monday morning, however, came the cheering news that General Sherman's army was again in motion, and had completed the crossing of the Chattahoochee River the evening before.

On the 19th they learned that General Sherman had established his lines within five miles of Atlanta, and that the Confederate general Johnston had been relieved by General Hood.

The messages by flag were received every day, when the weather was favorable, between the hours of nine and ten in the morning; and now that the campaign had reopened with such promise of continued activity, the days, and even the nights, dragged, so feverish was the desire of the soldiers to hear more. They wandered about the mountain-top and discussed the military situation; but, if anything more than another tended to soothe their nerves, it was the sight of their garden, in which the corn and potatoes were so far advanced that each day seemed to add visibly to their growth.

On the morning of the 21st they learned that Hood had assaulted that flank of the intrenched line which was commanded by General Hooker, and that in so doing the enemy had been three times gallantly repulsed. The new Confederate general was less prudent than the old one, and they chuckled to think of the miles of log breastworks they knew so well, at which he was hurling his troops. General Sherman was their military idol, and they knew how well satisfied he would be with this change in the tactics of the enemy.

By this time it had become their habit to remain near the station while Lieutenant Coleman figured out the messages, each of which he read aloud as soon as he comprehended its meaning.

On Saturday morning, July 23, while Corporal Bromley leaned stolidly on his flagstaff, and Philip walked about impatiently, Lieutenant Coleman jumped up and read from the paper he held in his hand:

"Hood attacked again yesterday. Repulsed with a loss of seven thousand killed and wounded."

With no thought of the horrible meaning of these formidable figures to the widows and orphans of the men who had fallen in this gallant charge, Philip and Bromley cheered and cheered again, while the lieutenant sat down to decipher the next message. When he had mastered it the paper fell from his hands. He was speechless for the moment.

"What is it?" said Philip, turning pale with the certainty of bad news.

"General McPherson is killed," said Lieutenant Coleman.

Now, so strangely are the passions of men wrought up in the time of war that these three hot-headed young partizans were quick to shed tears over the death of one man, though the destruction of a great host of their enemies had filled their hearts only with a fierce delight.

During the Sunday which followed there was a feeling of gloomy foreboding on the mountain, and under it a fierce desire to hear what should come next.

On Monday morning, July 25, the sun rose in a cloudless sky, bathing the trees and all the distant peaks with cheerful light, while at the altitude of the station his almost vertical rays were comfortable to feel in the cool breeze which blew across the plateau. Lieutenant Coleman glanced frequently at the face of his watch, and the instant the hands stood at nine Philip began waving the flag. There was no response from the other mountain for so long a time that Corporal Bromley came to his relief, and the red flag with a white center continued to beat the air with a rushing and fluttering sound which was painful in the silence and suspense of waiting.

When at last the little flag appeared on the object-glass of the telescope, it spelled but seven words and then disappeared. Philip uttered an exclamation of surprise at the brevity of the message, while Bromley wiped the perspiration from his forehead and waited where he stood.

In another minute Lieutenant Coleman had translated the seven words, but even in that brief time Corporal Bromley, whose eyes were fixed on his face, detected the deathly pallor which spread over his features. The young officer looked with a hopeless stare at his corporal, and without uttering a word extended his hand with the scrap of paper on which he had written the seven words of the message.

Bromley took it, while Philip ran eagerly forward and looked tremblingly over his comrade's shoulder.

The seven words of the message read:

"*General Sherman was killed yesterday before Atlanta.*"

CHAPTER VII

IN WHICH THE THREE SOLDIERS MAKE A REMARKABLE RESOLUTION

LIEUTENANT COLEMAN, although stunned by the news conveyed by the seven words of the message, as soon as he could reopen communication with the other mountain, telegraphed back to Lieutenant Swann, in command of the tenth station:

"Is there no mistake in flagging General Sherman's death?"

It was late in the afternoon when the return message came, which read as follows:

"None. I have taken the same precaution to telegraph back to the station at Chattanooga.

"LIEUTENANT JAMES SWANN, U. S. A."

After this, and the terrible strain of waiting, Lieutenant Coleman and Corporal Bromley walked away in different directions on the mountain-top; and poor Philip, left alone, sat down on the ground and burst into tears over the death of his favorite general. He saw nothing but gloom and disaster in the future. What would the old army do without its brilliant leader?

And, sure enough, on the following morning came the news that the heretofore victorious army was falling back across the Chattahoochee; and another despatch confirmed the death of General Sherman, who had been riding along his lines with a single orderly when he was shot through the heart by a sharp-shooter of the enemy.

Every morning after that the three soldiers went up to the station at the appointed hour, expecting only bad news, and, without fail, only bad news came. They learned that the baffled army in and about Marietta was being reorganized by General Thomas; but the ray of hope was quenched in their hearts a few days later, when the news came that General Grant had met with overwhelming disaster before Richmond, and, like McClellan before him, was fighting his way back to his base of supplies at City Point.

One day—it was August 6—there came a message from the chief signal-office at Chattanooga directing them to remain at their posts, at all hazards, until further orders; and, close upon this, a report that General Grant's army was rapidly concentrating on Washington by way of the Potomac River.

They had no doubt that the swift columns of Lee were already in motion overland toward the National capital, and they were not likely to be many days behind the

"POOR PHILIP, LEFT ALONE, BURST INTO TEARS."

Federal army in concentrating at that point. Rumors of foreign intervention followed quick on the heels of this disheartening news, and on August 10 came a despatch which, being interpreted, read: "Yesterday, after a forced march of incredible rapidity, Longstreet's corps crossed the Upper Potomac near the Chain Bridge, and captured two forts to the north of Rock Creek Church. At daylight on August 9, after tearing up a section of the Baltimore and Ohio's tracks, a column of cavalry under Fitzhugh Lee captured a train-load of the government archives, bound for Philadelphia."

Thus on the very day when General Sherman was bombarding the city of Atlanta, and when everything was going well with the National cause elsewhere, these misguided young men were brought to the verge of despair by some mysterious agency which was cunningly falsifying the daily despatches. Nothing more melancholy can be conceived than the entries made at this time by Lieutenant Coleman in the station diary.

Returning to the entry of July 26, which was the day following that on which they had received information of the death of General Sherman, the unhappy officer writes:

"My men are intensely patriotic, and the despatch came to each of us like a personal blow. Its effect on my two men was an interesting study of character. Corporal Bromley is a Harvard man, having executive ability as well as education far above his humble rank, who entered the service of his country at the first call to arms without a thought for his personal advantage. He is a man of high courage, and if he has a fault, it is a too outspoken intolerance of the failures of his superiors. Private Welton is of a naturally refined and sensitive nature, and at first he seemed wholly cowed and broken in spirit. Bromley, on the other hand, as he strode away from the station, showed a countenance livid with rage.

"After supper, for we take our meals apart, I invited the men to my tent, and we sat out in the moonlight to discuss the probable situation. We talked of the overwhelming news until late in the evening, and then sat for a time in silence in the shadow of the chestnut-trees, looking out at the dazzling whiteness of the mountain-top before retiring, each to his individual sorrow."

In the entry for August 6, after commenting somewhat bitterly on the report of the defeat of the Army of the Potomac, Lieutenant Coleman says, with reference to the despatch from the chief signal-officer of the same date:

"The situation at this station is such, owing to our ignorance of the sentiment of the mountaineers and the hazard of visiting them in uniform, that I find a grave difficulty confronting me, which must be provided for at once. Our guide to this point has returned to Tennessee with the cavalry escort, and I have now reason deeply to regret that he was not required to put us in communication with some trustworthy Union men. The issue of commissary stores is reduced from this date to half-rations, and we shall begin at once to eke out our daily portion by such edibles as we can find on the mountain. Huckleberries are abundant in the field above the bridge, and the men are already counting on the wild mandrakes.

"August 8. Nothing cheering to brighten the gloom of continued defeat and disaster. The necessity of procuring everything edible within our reach keeps my men busy and affords them something to think of besides the disasters to the National armies. Welton discovered to-day four fresh-laid eggs, snugly hidden in a nest of leaves, under a clump of chestnut sprouts, interwoven with dry grasses, three of which he brought in."

These entries referring to trivial things are interesting as showing the temper of the men, and how they employed their time at this critical period.

On August 18 came a despatch that the Army of Northern Virginia was entering Washington without material opposition. Lieutenant Coleman, in a portion of his diary for this date, says:

"After a prolonged state of anger, during which he has commented bitterly on the conduct of affairs at Washington, Corporal Bromley has settled into a morose and irritable mood, in which no additional disaster disturbs him in the slightest degree. With his fine perceptions and well-trained mind, the natural result of a liberal education, I have found him heretofore a most interesting companion in hours off duty. My situation is made doubly intolerable by his present condition."

At 9:30 A. M. of August 20, 1864, came the last despatches that were received by the three soldiers on Whiteside Mountain.

"Hold on for immediate relief. Peace declared. Confederate States are to retain Washington."

The effect of this last message upon the young men who received it is fully set forth in the diary of the following day, and no later account could afford so vivid a picture of the remarkable events recorded by Lieutenant Coleman:

"August 21, 1864. The messages of yesterday were flagged with the usual precision, and we have no reason to doubt their accuracy. Indeed, what has happened was expected by us so confidently that the despatches as translated by me were received in silence by my men and without any evidence of excitement or surprise. I myself felt a sense of relief that the inevitable and disgraceful end had come.

. . . . . .

"Last evening was a memorable occasion to the three men on this mountain. We are no longer separated by any difference in rank, having mutually agreed to waive all such conditions. In presence of such agreement, I, Frederick Henry Coleman, Second Lieutenant in the 12th Regiment of Cavalry of the military forces of the United States (formerly so called), have this day, August 21, 1864, written my resignation and sealed and addressed it to the Adjutant-General, wherever he may be. I am fully aware that, until the document is forwarded to its destination, only some power outside myself can terminate my official connection with the army, and that my personal act operates only to divest me of rank in the estimation of my companions in exile.

"After our supper last night we walked across the field in front of our quarters and around to the point where the northern end of the plateau joins the rocky face of the mountain. The sun had already set behind the opposite ridge, and the gathering shadows among the rocks and under the trees added a further color of melancholy to our gloomy and foreboding thoughts.

"I am forced to admit that I have not been the dominant spirit in the resolution at which we have arrived. George Bromley had several times asserted that he would never return to a disgraced and divided country. At the time I had regarded his words as only the irresponsible expression of excitement and passion.

"As we stood together on the hill last night, Bromley reverted to this subject, speaking with unusual calmness and deliberation. 'For my part,' said he, pausing to give force to his decision, 'I never desire to set foot in the United States again. I suppose I am as well equipped for the life of a hermit as any other man; and I am sure that my temper is not favorable to meeting my countrymen, who are my countrymen no longer, and facing the humiliation and disgrace of this defeat. I have no near relatives and no personal attachments to compensate for what I regard as the sacrifice of a return and a tacit acceptance of the new order of things. I came into the army fresh from a college course which marked the close of my youth; and shall I return in disgrace, without a profession or ambition, to begin a new career in the shadow of this overwhelming disaster? I bind no one to my resolution,' he continued in clear, cold tones; 'all I ask is that you leave me the old flag, and I will set up a country of my own on this mountain-top, whose natural defenses will enable me to keep away all disturbers of my isolation.'

"I was deeply impressed with his words, and the more so because of the absence of all passion in his manner. I had respected him for his attainments; I now felt that I loved the man for his unselfish, consuming love of country. Strange to say, I, too, was without ties of kindred. My best friends in the old army had fallen in battle for the cause that was lost. On the night when we sat together exulting over the double victory of the capture of Kenesaw Mountain and the sinking of the 'Alabama,' I had expressed a determination to renounce my chosen profession in a certain event. That event had taken place. Under the magnetic influence of Bromley, what had only been a threat before became a bitter impulse and then a fierce resolve.

"Taking his hand and looking steadily into his calm eyes, I said: 'I am an officer of the United States army, but I will promise you this: until I am ordered to do so, I will never leave this place.'

A REMARKABLE RESOLUTION

"Philip Welton had been a silent listener to this strange conversation. His more sentimental nature was melted to tears, and in a few words he signified his resolution to join his fate with ours.

"We walked back across the mountain-top in the white light of the full moon, silently as we had come. After the resolve we had made, I began already to experience a sense of relief from the shame I felt at the failure of our numerous armies. The old government had fallen from its proud position among the nations of the earth. The flag we loved had been trampled under foot and despoiled of its stars—of how many we knew not. Our path lay through the plantation of young corn, whose broad, glistening leaves brushed our faces and filled the air with the sweet fragrance of the juicy stalks. The planting seemed to have been an inspiration which alone would make it possible for us to survive the first winter."

CHAPTER VIII

WHICH ENDS IN A BATTLE

THE morning after the three soldiers had pledged themselves to a life of exile, like the (otherwise) practical young persons they were, they proceeded resolutely to take stock of the provisions they had on hand and to consider the means of adding to their food-supply. They had already been nearly two months in camp, which was the period for which their rations had been issued; but, what with the generous measure of the government and the small game they had brought down with their carbines, nearly half of the original supply remained on storage in the hut of the old man of the mountain. It is true that there was but one box left of the hard bread; but the salt beef, which had been covered with brine in the cask found in the corner of the cabin, had scarcely been touched. A few strips of the bacon still hung from the rafters. Of the peas and beans, only a few scattering seeds lay here and there on the floor. The precious salt formed but a small pile by itself, but there was still a brave supply of coffee and sugar, and the best part of the original package of rice. In another month they would have green corn and potatoes of their own growing, and they already had eggs, as, fortunately, they had killed none of their hens.

The tract of ground on the mountain was a half-hundred acres in extent, with an abundance of wood and water, protected on the borders by trees and bushes, and accessible only by the wooden ladder by which they themselves had come up the ledge. Their camp was in the center of the tract, where the smoke of their fires would never be seen from the valleys. Overhanging the boulder face of the mountain, just back of the ridge they had used for a signal-station, was a clump of black oaks, through which something like an old trail led down to a narrow tongue of land caught on a shelf of granite, which was dark with a tall growth of pines, and the earth beneath was covered with a thick, gray carpet of needles, clean and springy to the feet. Along the southern cliff, and to the west of the spring which welled out from under the rock, was a curtain of dogwoods and birches, and elsewhere the timber was chestnut. At some points the trees of the latter variety were old and gnarled, and clung to the rocks by fantastic twisted roots like the claws of great birds, and at others they grew in thrifty young groves, three and four lusty trunks springing from the sides of a decayed stump.

They were certainly in the heart of the Confederacy, but the plateau was theirs by the right of possession, and over this, come what might, they were determined that the old flag with its thirty-five stars should continue to float. They at least would stubbornly refuse to acknowledge that there had been any change in the number of States.

Owing to the danger of being seen, they agreed together that no one should go down the ladder during the day. They were satisfied that they had not been seen since they had occupied the mountain. They had no reason to believe that any human being had crossed the bridge since the night the captain and his troopers had ridden away into the darkness; but still the bridge remained, the only menace to their safety, and, with the military instinct of a small army retreating in an enemy's country, they determined to destroy that means of reaching them.

Accordingly, when night came, Lieutenant Coleman and George Bromley, leaving Philip asleep in the hut, armed themselves with the ax and the two carbines, and took their way across the lower field to the deep gorge. They had not been there since the night they parted with the captain and Andy, the guide. It was very still in this secluded place—even stiller, they thought, for the ceaseless tinkling of the branch in the bottom of the gorge. They had grown quite used to the stillness and solitude of nature in that upper wilderness. Enough of moonlight fell through the branches overhead so that they could see the forms of the trees that grew in the gorge; and the moon itself was so low in the west that its rays slanted under the bridge and touched with a ghostly light the dead top of a great basswood which forked its giant limbs upward like beckoning arms. Then there was one ray of light that lanced its way to the very heart of the gorge, and touched a tiny patch of sparkling water alongside a shining rock.

They had the smallest ends of the string-pieces to deal with, as the trees had fallen from the other side. Bromley wielded the ax, which fell at first with a muffled sound in the rotten log, and then, as he reached the tougher heart, rang out clear and sharp, and echoed back from down the gorge. Presently he felt a weakening in the old stick, and, stepping back, he wiped his forehead on the sleeve of his jacket. The stillness which followed the blows of the ax was almost startling; and the night wind which was rising on the mountain sounded like the rushing of wings in the tops of the pines on the opposite bank.

After another moment's rest, Corporal Bromley laid his ax to the other string-piece. Lieutenant Coleman had taken position a few yards below the bridge, with his arm around a young chestnut, where he could detect the first movement of the swaying timbers. Fragments of bark and rotten wood were shaken from the crazy structure at every stroke of the ax, and a tiny chipmunk sprang out of his home in the stones, frightened at the chopping, and fled with light leaps across the doomed causeway. Now the blows fall more slowly, and after each stroke the axman steps back to listen. At last he hears a measured crackling in the resinous heart of the old log. He hears earth and small stones dropping from the abutment into the branches of the trees below. The structure lurches to one side; there is a sound like a dull explosion; a few loose sticks dance in the yellow cloud of dust that rises thick and stifling from the broken banks, and the toilsome work of thirty years before is undone in as many minutes.

When the dust-cloud had drifted off, our two heroes, who had retreated for safety, came cautiously back and looked over into the gorge. They were startled at what they saw; for the frame of the old bridge was poised in the moonlight like Mohammed's coffin, and swaying mockingly, as if the soul of the old man of the mountain had taken refuge in its timbers. Its slivered planks stood up like the fins of some sea-monster, crisscrossed and trembling, and spread out like the broken sticks of a fan.

"Good!" said Lieutenant Coleman; "it has lodged in the forked arms of the dead basswood; and the mountain people will attach some mystery to its going, as they did to its coming."

He said "Good!" because the more mystery there was between their retreat and the enemy outside, the better. It would be many a long year now before anybody would be likely to come to disturb them; and with this thought in their hearts, they slung their carbines and took the way back.

When they had come as far as the hollow tree into which the cartridges had been thrown on the first night to keep them from the rain, they halted; and George Bromley felt of the edge of the ax as he measured the height of the opening above the ground with his eye. He was not quite satisfied with this kind of measurement, and so, leaning against the old trunk, he thrust his right arm to its full length into the broad, black cavity. He was about to touch with his fingers the spot outside, opposite to which his right hand reached, when something like an exclamation of anger fell from his lips, and he lifted out of the opening a bear cub as large as a woodchuck. Bromley's bare hand had landed unexpectedly in the soft fur of the animal, and, with an absence of fear peculiar to himself, he had closed his powerful grip on the unknown object, and lifted out the young bear by the nape of its neck. Strong as he was, he was unable to hold the squirming cub until he had turned it over on its back and planted his knee on its chest.

Behind the tree there was a great, dark hole among the rocks, which was the real entrance to the bears' den; and expecting an attack from that quarter, Lieutenant Coleman stood quietly in the moonlight, with his thumb on the lock of his carbine. As there was no movement anywhere, he presently returned to the hole in the tree, and prudently thrust in his short gun, which he worked about until the broad, flat end of the hinged ramrod was entangled in the coarse meshes of the sack. The cartridges were bone-dry after seven weeks in the bears' den, and the young cub was thrust into the bag, where he growled and struggled against the unknown power that was bearing him off.

They had neither chains nor cage nor strong boxes, and when they had come safely back to the cabin with their prize they were greatly puzzled as to how they should secure it for the night. Philip was sleeping soundly on a bed of boughs in one corner, and showed no disposition to wake. They were careful not to disturb him, wishing to prepare a pleasant surprise for him when he should wake in the morning and find the captured cub.

"I have it," said Bromley, when his eyes had traveled around the room to the fireplace; "the cub can't climb up the smooth stones of the chimney, and we will find a way to shut it in by blocking up the fireplace."

They unslung the door of the cabin from its wooden hinges, and, after slipping the young bear from the mouth of the sack into the soft ashes, they quickly closed the opening, and secured the door in place, putting the meat-cask against one end and a heavy stone against the other.

After a little disturbance in the ashes all was quiet in the fireplace. Lieutenant Coleman went away to his tent, and in five minutes after he lay down George Bromley was fast asleep beside Philip.

At this time the moon was shining in at the open door; but shortly afterward it set behind the western ridges, and in the hour before daybreak it was unusually dark on the mountain. Bromley was sleeping more lightly than usual, and, following his experience of the night, he was dreaming of desperate encounters with bears; or this may have happened because the cub in the chimney from time to time put his small nose to a hole in the door and whined, and then growled as he fell back into the ashes.

One of the light cracker-boxes stood on end just inside the door, and it was the noise of this object thrown over on the floor that startled Bromley in the midst of his dream, just at the point where he saw the bear approach-

THE MOTHER BEAR COMES FOR HER CUB.

ing. He was awake in an instant, but the spell of the dream was still on him, and he wondered that, instead of the huge form of the bear of his sleep, he saw only two glittering eyes in the doorway. For an instant he was at a loss to tell where he was. He saw the grayish opening of the window in the surrounding blackness, and a peculiar hole in the roof not quite covered by the pieces of shelter-tent; and just as he came to himself the cub in the chimney, smelling its mother, whined joyfully at the hole in the door. With a deep growl the old bear scrambled over the creaking floor to her young one. Instinctively Bromley put out his hand for his carbine, and then he remembered that both guns had been left lying on the stone hearth. At the same time Philip awoke with a start, and the she-bear, scenting her natural enemies, uttered a growl which was half a snarl, and was about to charge into the corner where they lay, when Bromley snatched the blankets and threw them so dexterously over the gleaming eyes that in the momentary confusion of the brute he had time to drag and push Philip through the open door and out of the cabin.

Furious as the beast was, she had no disposition to follow the boys into the open air. Her natural instinct kept her in the neighborhood of her imprisoned offspring, where she sat heavily on the two carbines and growled fiercely. The bear now had full and undisputed possession of the cabin, as well as of the entire stock of firearms, which absurd advantage she held until daylight, while Bromley and Philip sat impatiently in the lower limbs of an old chestnut, where they had promptly taken refuge. Bromley had secured the ax in his retreat, and while Philip sat securely above him, he guarded the approach along the sloping trunk, and would have welcomed the bear right gladly. They were near enough to throw sticks upon the "A" tent, and before daylight Lieutenant Coleman was awakened and was lodged in the branches with them.

"How very fortunate!" said Philip from the top of the tree. "We shall have a supply of jerked bear's meat for the winter."

"Not so long as the bear sits on the carbines," said Bromley, with a grim smile.

"If we could get that young cub out of the chimney—" said Lieutenant Coleman.

"Or the old bear into it," suggested Philip.

"Either way," said the lieutenant, "would put us in possession of the guns, and decide the battle in our favor."

By the time they had, in their imaginations, dressed the bear and tanned her skin, it began to be light enough to enter upon a more vigorous and offensive campaign. This idea seemed to strike the bear at the same time, for she came out of the door, and, after sniffing the morning air, shambled three times around the cabin, smelling and clawing at the base of the chimney in each passage. Having made this survey of her surroundings, she returned to her post and lay down on the carbines.

These carbines were old smooth-bore muskets cut down for cavalry arms and fitted with a short bar and sliding ring over the lock-plate, which was stamped "Tower—

London, 1862." They carried a ball fixed in front of a paper cartridge, and were fired by means of a percussion-cap. The pieces were loaded where they lay, with caps under the locks.

There was a crevice between the logs at that side of the chimney where the door was held in position by the stone, and the wooden spade which Philip had used in his planting could be seen from where the three soldiers sat in the tree, lying across the grave of the old man of the mountain. Lieutenant Coleman and Bromley slipped down to the ground and ran around to the back of the hut. The end of the door could be seen against the crevice, which was just above the level of the floor. The men took care to keep close to the chimney, so as to be out of sight of the bear, and when they had fixed their lever under the edge of the door they easily raised it high enough to let out the cub.

When this was done they mounted to the roof of the cabin, Coleman armed with the wooden spade and Bromley with the ax. The bear came out presently, with the cub at her side, its thick fur gray with ashes. The two were headed to pass between the tent and the chestnut-tree, and when the old bear stopped at the foot of the trunk and raised her head with a threatening growl, Bromley stood up on the roof and hurled the ax, which slightly wounded the bear in the flank and caused her to charge back toward the cabin, while the bewildered cub scrambled up the tree in which Philip sat.

Philip only laughed and called loudly to his comrades

to get the guns. At the sound of his voice the she-bear turned about, and, seeing her cub in the tree, began scrambling up after it. At this quite unexpected turn in affairs Philip began to climb higher, no longer disposed to laugh, while Bromley jumped down on the opposite side of the cabin and secured the carbines, one of which he passed up to Lieutenant Coleman on the roof. Now, Coleman had a clear eye and a steady hand with a gun, and would have hit the heart of the bear with his bullet like the handiest old sport of the woods, but as the animal crouched in the crotch of the tree a great limb covered her side and head. By this time Philip was as high as he dared to climb. The cub from the ashes was hugging the same slender limb, breathing on his naked feet, and the old bear, with bristling hair and erect ears, was growling where she lay, and putting out her great claws to go aloft after Philip. This was the critical moment, when Bromley ran under the tree and shot the bear. His ball went crashing into her shoulder instead of between the ribs behind, as he had meant it should. It was just as well, he thought, when he saw her come rolling along the trunk to the ground as if she were thrice dead. If he had only known bears a little better, he would probably have exchanged carbines and kept a safe distance from the animal; and even then, in the end, it might have been worse for him.

He had only broken her big, shaggy shoulder, and as he came near to the wounded brute she rose suddenly on her hind feet and dealt him such a whack with her sound paw as nearly broke his ribs and sent him rolling over

"SHE ROSE SUDDENLY ON HER HIND FEET AND DEALT HIM SUCH A WHACK AS NEARLY BROKE HIS RIBS."

and over on the ground. Bear and man were so mixed in the air that even Coleman feared to risk a shot. Poor Bromley, crippled and bleeding at the nose, lay almost helpless on his back under the tree, and in this state the maddened bear charged furiously on him, her foaming and bloody jaws extended. Half stunned and more than half beaten, he had retained his cool nerve and a firm grip on his empty carbine; and as the bear came over him, with all his remaining strength he crushed the clumsy weapon into her open mouth like a huge bit. She was so near that he felt her hot breath on his face, and saw her flaming eyes through the blood which nearly blinded his own. Bromley felt his strength going. The breath was nearly crushed out of his body by the weight of the bear, baffled for an instant by the mass of iron between her jaws. Philip, drawing up his toes from the cub, forgot his own peril as he gazed down in terror at the struggle below. At the moment which he believed was Bromley's last a quick report rang out from the roof, and the great bear rolled heavily to one side, with Lieutenant Coleman's bullet in her heart.

It is not to be supposed that in the excitement of destroying bridges and killing bears Lieutenant Coleman neglected the signal-station. Morning after morning they waved their flag, and watched the summit of Upper Bald through the glass. No one could be more eager than were the three soldiers without a country to hear some further news of the old government they had loved and lost. They even turned their attention to Chestnut Knob. The entries in the diary show that this duty was continued hopelessly through September, with no reply to their signals from either mountain.

That disaster had overtaken the armies of the United States they accepted as a fact, and busied themselves about their domestic affairs that they might, being occupied, the more easily forget their great disappointment. The flesh of the bear was cured in long strips by the cool air and hot sun. To protect themselves from another unwelcome surprise, they removed the short upper ladder from the ledge in the cliff, and the bear cub, which had become a great pet under the name of "Tumbler," was allowed the range of the plateau.

In this month of September the soldier exiles built a comfortable new house on ground a little in front of the old hut. Its walls were constructed of chestnut logs cut from the grove to the west, where they could be easily rolled down the hill, after which they were scored with the ax on the inner side, and notched so as to fit quite closely together. The roof was made of rafters and flattened string-pieces, and covered with shingles which they split from short sections of oak, and which were held in place with the nails that had been provided for the station. The floor was of pounded clay, raised a foot above the ground outside. It was a prodigious labor to bring down on rollers the great flat stone which they dug out of the hillside for the fireplace. After this was laid firmly for a hearth, they built the chimney outside, laying the stones in a mortar of clay until the throat was sufficiently narrow; and after that they carried the flue above the ridge-pole with sticks thickly plastered with mud. The house had two windows under the eaves opposite to each other; and the doorway, which was in the gable end facing the fireplace, was fitted with the door from the old cabin, which they had no doubt had been framed down the mountain, and brought up by Josiah after midnight, and most likely it had been paid for with some of the strange gold pieces which had excited the suspicion of the gossips in the valley.

It was a wonderfully comfortable house to look at, and almost made them long for the fall rain to beat on the roof, and for the cold nights when they could build a fire in the great chimney.

CHAPTER IX

THE PLATEAU RECEIVES A NAME

IT was now October, and time to being harvesting the crop on the little plantation, which something very like an inspiration had prompted Philip to plant. While Lieutenant Coleman continued work on the house, stopping the chinks between the logs with clay, and repairing the roof of the hut with spare shingles, Bromley and Philip "topped" the corn, cutting off the stalks above the ripened ears. Then the potatoes were thrown out of the mellow soil with a wooden shovel, and left to dry in the sun, while a level place was prepared in the center of the plot, and thickly spread with a carpet of dry stalks. Upon this surface, after removing a few bushels to the hut, the crop was gathered into a conical heap and thatched over with stalks, and then the whole was thickly covered with earth and trenched about to turn off the water.

It was estimated that this cache contained thirty bushels, which, according to the table in the Blue Book (Revised

Army Regulations), would exceed the potato ration of three men for a period of five years.

From the day of their arrival on the mountain, Lieutenant Coleman had never failed to make a daily entry in the station journal; and now that they had set up a country for themselves, he foresaw that the continuance of this practice would be necessary if they were not to lose the record of weeks and months. His entry was always brief. Often it was no more than the date, and even the more important events were set down with the utmost brevity and precision.

Once a week he noted the recurrence of the Sabbath, and on that day they suspended ordinary labor, and, if the weather was pleasant, inspected their increasing domestic comforts on the mountain-top and laid their plans for the future. After their military habit, the morning of Sunday was devoted to personal cleanliness and to tidying up about their quarters.

As the commissary supply of yellow bars diminished, it was evident that the time would soon come when they should be obliged to make their own soap. Back of the chestnut-tree in which they had taken refuge from the bear was a peculiar hollowed rock, and above it a flat shelf of stone, on which Philip erected a hollow log for leaching ashes. A little patient chipping of the upper stone with the ax-head made a shallow furrow along which the lye would trickle from the leach, and fall into the natural basin in the rock below, which was large enough to hold a half-barrel. This was a happy device, as the strong liquid would have eaten its way through any vessel other than an iron pot or an earthen jar, of which unfortunately they possessed neither.

They had but a limited supply of hard corn, from which they selected the best ears for the next year's planting. These they braided together by the husks, and hung up in yellow festoons from the rafters of the hut, which they continued to use as a storehouse. Much of what remained of their small crop would be needed by the fowls in the winter, and up to this time they had made no use of it for their own food.

Meal was out of the question, and to break the flinty kernels between stones was a tedious process to which they had not yet been forced to resort.

The presence of the lye, however, suggested to Bromley the hulled corn of his New England grandmother, which he had seen her prepare by soaking and boiling the kernels in a thin solution of lye. By this means the hulls or skins were removed, and after cleansing from potash, and boiling all day, the unbroken kernels became as white and tender as rice.

This satisfied the three soldiers for a time, and made an agreeable addition to their diet of bear steak and potatoes. In the mountains of Tennessee Lieutenant Coleman had once seen a rude hydraulic contrivance called a Slow-John, which was a sort of lazy man's mill. To construct this affair it was necessary to have a bucket, which Bromley set about making by the slow process of burning out a section of chestnut log with the red-hot ramrod of a carbine.

At a short distance above the house, the branch which flowed from the spring, after making its refreshing way between grassy banks, tumbled over a succession of ledges which ended in a small cascade, and twelve feet below this waterfall there was a broad, flat rock which laved its mossy sides in the branch, and showed a clean, flat surface above the level of the water. Below this rock they built a dam of stones, by means of which they could flood its surface.

Four feet up-stream from the rock a log was fixed from bank to bank for a fulcrum, and upon this rested a movable lever, the short arm of which terminated above the submerged rock, while the long arm just touched the water of the cascade. A wooden pin set in the under log passed through a slot in the lever, so as to hold it in position and at the same time give it free play. Another flat stone of about thirty pounds' weight, which was the pestle of the mortar, was lashed with grape-vine thongs to the short arm of the lever directly over the submerged stone. To the long arm was attached Bromley's bucket, bailed with a strong wire, and so hung as to catch the water of the cascade. As the bucket filled and sank, its weight raised the flat stone higher and higher above the submerged rock until the bucket met a bar fixed to tilt its contents into the stream, when the upper millstone came down upon its fellow with a fine splash and thud. After a wall of clay had been built about the surface where the two stones met, to keep the corn in place, the Slow-John was ready for work.

It was slow, but it was sure, and after that, when one

of the three soldiers awoke in the night, it was cheerful to hear the regular splash and crash of the Slow-John, like the ticking of a huge clock, lazy enough to tick once a minute, and patient enough to keep on ticking for two days and nights to pulverize as many quarts of corn.

And now, for three young men who had solemnly renounced their country and cut themselves off voluntarily from all intercourse with their kind, they were about as cheerful and contented as could be expected. In spite of the great disaster which they believed had befallen the National cause, their lungs expanded in the rare mountain air, and the good red blood danced in their veins, and with youth and health of body it was impossible to take an altogether gloomy view of life. They had at first tried hard to be miserable, but nature was against them, and the effort had been a failure. In their free life they could no more resist the infection of happiness than the birds in the trees could refrain from singing, and so it came to pass that in view of the bountiful harvest they had gathered, and the comfortable house they had built, and all the domestic conveniences they had contrived, Lieutenant Coleman came out boldly in favor of setting apart Thursday, the twenty-fourth day of November, as a Day of Thanksgiving, and quite forgot to name it a day of humiliation as well. To this the others joyfully agreed, and agreed, moreover, that from that day forward the plateau should be called Lincoln Territory in memory of the patriotism of the good President, notwithstanding they felt that his divided counselors and incompetent generals had wiped the half of a great nation from the map of the world.

When this first holiday dawned on the mountain, the three soldiers arrayed themselves in full uniform for the ceremony of naming their possessions. Bromley and Philip buckled on their cavalry swords and slung their carbines at their backs, and Lieutenant Coleman, for the last time, assumed his discarded rank to take command. The arms had been polished the day before until they gleamed and flashed in the morning light, and the little army of two was dressed and faced and inspected, and then left at parade-rest while Lieutenant Coleman brought out the flag. How their honest hearts swelled with pride to think that here, alone in all the world, that flag would continue to float with an undiminished field of stars! Little did they dream that on that very morning hundreds like it were waving in the heart of Georgia over Sherman's legions on their march to the sea. When at last it blew out from the staff, they gathered under its folds, and sang "The Star-spangled Banner" with tears in their eyes; and as the last words of the good old song rang out over the mountain-top, Philip and Bromley discharged their carbines, and all three cheered lustily for the old flag and the new name.

This was to be their last military ceremony, and having no further use for their swords, they arranged them with belts and scabbards into a handsome decoration against the chimneypiece, and crossed above them the three red-and-white flags of the station. The Revised Army Regulations and Philip's prayer-book stood on the mantelpiece alongside the spy-glass in its leathern case. The few articles of extra clothing hung in a line on the wall just opposite to the three bunks, whose under layer of pine boughs gave an aromatic perfume to the room.

After the ceremony of naming the plateau, and having fixed the trophies to their satisfaction, the three exiles took down their sky-blue overcoats from the line, for the November air was nipping cold, and set out with the two carbines and an empty sack to keep Thanksgiving in the good old country way. They were still rather sad after what had happened in the morning; but by the time they were back all the gloom had worn off, for they brought with them two rabbits and a bag of chestnuts, and appetites sharpened by exercise in the keen air.

Philip made the stew, and Bromley fried two chickens of their own raising, one after the other, on a half-canteen, and the potatoes, left to themselves, burst their jackets in the ashes with impatience to be eaten. Each man made his own coffee in his own blackened tin cup, and drank it with a keener relish because it was near the last of their commissary stock.

While they were eating and drinking within, the sky without had become thick with clouds blown up on the east wind, so that when they looked out at the door they saw Tumbler, the bear, who also had been stuffing himself with acorns, and ants which he had pawed out of a rotten log, rolling home for shelter.

There was yet time before the storm broke, and away

CHRISTENING THE TERRITORY.

they went up the hill as happy as lords, to load themselves with dead chestnut limbs and a few resinous sticks of fat pine; and when night came, and with it the rain, there was a warm fire in the new chimney, and a stick of lightwood thrust behind the backlog lighted the interior of the house with a good forty-adamantine-candle power. Tumbler lay rolled up in his favorite corner, blinking his small eyes at the unusual light, and from time to time he passed his furry paw over his sharp nose and gave forth a low grunt of satisfaction. Philip sat against the chimney opposite Tumbler, stirring chestnuts in the ashes with a ramrod, while Bromley put away the last of the supper things, and Lieutenant Coleman gazed out of the open window into the slanting rain, which beat a merry tattoo on the shingles, and tossed at intervals a sturdy drop on the hissing fire.

It was certainly not the cheerful interior, beaming with light and heat, that turned Lieutenant Coleman's thoughts back to the dark cloud of disasters which had overwhelmed the National arms; it might have been the dismal outlook from the square window into the darkness and the storm. At all events, he turned abruptly about as if a new idea had struck him.

"George, this sudden success of the Johnnies has not been gained without important outside aid. The French in Mexico may have decided at last to cross the border, and if they did it was in concert with the naval demonstrations of more than one European power against the blockade."

"That is just what I have been thinking, Fred," said Bromley, "and England is sure to be at the bottom of it. After the sinking of the 'Alabama' there was no time to be lost, and when Grant's army began to fall back from Richmond, that hostile government had the excuse it had long been waiting for, and recognized the Confederacy at once."

"I am of the opinion," replied Lieutenant Coleman, thoughtfully, "that the recognition of the European powers came before the withdrawal from Richmond, because Grant would never have yielded that position except in obedience to orders from Washington. Now would he?"

"No, he wouldn't," said Bromley.

"Of course not," said Philip. "It all began with the death of Uncle Billy."

"So it did," said Bromley; "and after Sherman's army was out of the way Johnston probably joined his forces with Hood, defeated Thomas, and retook Chattanooga. He could hardly have accomplished all that by August 20, but his cavalry must have struck our line of stations on that date."

"Exactly so, George," Lieutenant Coleman responded. "If they had captured the tenth station alone, with Captain Swann, the line would have been useless and no further messages could have reached us. If Swann had found the line broken behind him, he would certainly have flagged that news to me without delay."

"Well, what's the odds?" said Philip, drawing his chestnuts out upon the hearthstone. "The jig was up, and Captain Swann knew it. If they had taken any station this side of the tenth mountain, the effect to us would have been the same."

"So it would," said Lieutenant Coleman, sadly, turning again to look out into the storm—"so it would."

"It is a blessing that we are ignorant of some things that have happened," said Bromley, who was disposed to look on the dark side. "It would have been just like Lee's impudence, after Washington was garrisoned, to cut loose with his army, and live on the country through Maryland, Pennsylvania, and New Jersey until he reached his foreign allies in the port of New York. If he has done that, for instance, I should rather not know it. Well," continued Bromley, "there is one comfort: if the Rebs conquer everything, they will defeat their own purpose and reestablish the Union they sought to destroy."

"Yes," said Lieutenant Coleman, "but it would be a Union with slavery everywhere. They can turn the Northern States back into Territories, and carry slavery into Massachusetts."

"Bah!" exclaimed Philip. "To think of the Territory of Ohio! The Territory of Pennsylvania! The Territory of New York!"

"Dear me!" said Lieutenant Coleman; "it is all too humiliating to think of. After all, what a miserable figure Abraham Lincoln will cut in history! Think of it! His Emancipation Proclamation is not worth the paper it was written on!"

"Ten thousand furies!" cried Bromley, striding across

the earthen floor and kicking the logs until the fire danced in the chimney; "we made a wise choice when we determined to stay on this mountain."

"But we did make a mistake when we named the plateau Lincoln Territory," cried Philip.

"That's so," said Bromley and Lieutenant Coleman, with one voice.

"It's not too late yet," shouted Bromley. "Sherman! Sherman was the only general worthy the name."

And they all cried "Sherman! Sherman!" and by common consent, after all the ceremony of the morning, the name of the plateau was changed to SHERMAN TERRITORY.

CHAPTER X

THE PRISONERS

THE ledge up which the ladders led from the direction of the gorge, it will be remembered, formed the northern support of the plateau. The unscalable cliff terminated its extent to the south; and of the two longer sides the one on the west overlooked Whiteside Cove, and that on the east Cashiers valley. The view into the Cove over the boulder side of the mountain, after the trees which grew on the edge were reached, was broad and unobstructed. On the eastern side there was but one gap in the timber which covered the mountain-side from the end of the ledge to the cliff, through which a perfect view could be had of the settlement in the valley. Before Andy Zachary left the plateau, Lieutenant Coleman had sketched a rude plot of the mountains overlooking the valley, and at the guide's dictation had written down the name of each peak. Yellow Mountain was the nearest, and showed a dark, timbered ridge beyond the gorge. At the northern end of the valley rose the mass of Sheep Cliff, and joined to it were the lesser ridges of Big and Little Terrapin. Hog's Back showed its blue top ten miles away to the east, beyond the nearer wooded ridges that shut in the valley on that side, down to Rock Mountain and Chimney Top, which reared their sharp peaks to the right of the plateau. Directly below this eastern outlook lay the one white road which ran through the valley, the same road along which the cavalcade had picked its silent way in the small hours of the morning, five months before, when they had come, full of hope, to establish the station.

Our exiles up to this time had been so busy with their preparations for winter that they had given but little attention to their neighbors below. They had noticed on frosty mornings columns of white smoke rising straight into the air from half a dozen cabins in the valley, most of which had been hidden from view by the thick foliage during the summer months. Now that the November winds had stripped the trees of their leaves, two cabins appeared in the direction of Sheep Cliff, standing side by side among the bare oaks on a knoll which sloped gently to the road. The two seemed to be precisely alike, with rude verandas in front, and at no great distance back of these, in an open clearing, surrounded with orchards and stacks, was a long house with a heavy stone chimney at each end. Scattered to the right of the plateau were several cabins, and close on the road a square brown building which looked to be a store. Just below this point of rocks where the three soldiers looked down on the valley stood the largest house in the settlement, old and rambling in construction, with lurching chimneys and roofs extending to left and rear. The woodpile was at the opposite side of the road, and comfortable log barns stood on the hillside above. All these details were to be seen with the naked eye, but the powerful telescope of the station revealed much more, even showing the faces and forms of the people who lived in the cabins.

As the three exiles were lounging together one afternoon at this very point of rocks, studying their neighbors through the telescope as if they had been the inhabitants of another planet, Philip broke the silence with quite an original speech—one only he could make.

"See here, fellows," he said with that new familiarity they had begun to show toward each other, "as we are likely to take considerable interest in these people down below, it will be mighty inconvenient when we talk about them to say, 'The man in the big house across the road from the log barn did this,' or 'The man in the farthest twin cabin did that,' or 'The old chap in the long house flanked by orchards and stacks did something else'; so I say, let's give them family names."

The others laughingly admitted that the idea was not a bad one, and Bromley suggested at random the names Smith, Jones, and Brown.

"As good as any others," said Philip.

"Very well," said Bromley, "then we will call this first neighbor 'Smith.'"

"No, you don't," cried Philip, with much spirit. "I've taken a prejudice against that old fellow, because he sits on the woodpile and smokes his pipe every afternoon while his wife does the milking. Smith is too respectable a name for him."

"I did n't know," said Coleman, laughing, "that there was any particular virtue in the name of Smith."

"I did n't say there was," said Philip, "but if this first old loafer should turn out half as bad as I fear he will, the name would be a slur on too many families, you know. Now, if it 's all the same to you, gentlemen, we will begin at the other end and call the man of the orchard 'Smith.' 'Jones' naturally falls to the owner of the second twin cabin, and this fellow below becomes—say, 'Shifless,' whether he likes it or not."

As no one of the three had ever heard of any one of the name of Shifless, Philip's arrangement was agreed to, and from time to time they settled other names on the dwellers in every cabin in sight, and one column of smoke which rose from behind an intervening ridge was spoken of as "Thompson's smoke."

On the morning of December 23 in that first year on the mountain, the three soldiers were thrown into a great state of excitement by a remarkable discovery. Coleman and Bromley were clearing off the snow from a stack of peavines, preparatory to beating them out on the floor of the house, when Philip came running toward them, holding up the telescope and beckoning them to meet him. He said he had seen three United States officers at the long cabin under Sheep Cliff, which was known as Smith's. The others needed no urging to follow Philip. Indeed, they ran so rapidly over the frozen ground in the rare upper air that they scarcely had breath for speaking when they arrived on the point of rocks. Philip directed the glass on the house again, and then, with a cry of delight, he passed it to Coleman.

"There they are! There they are! See? By the end of the house!"

As soon as the lieutenant had adjusted the powerful glass to his eye, he had the men before him almost as distinctly as if they had been standing within hailing distance. There was no mistaking the evidence that two of them were officers of what the three soldiers considered the beaten and disbanded army, while, although the third was in citizen's dress, it was unlike the dress of the mountaineers.

"Heaven help them!" exclaimed Lieutenant Coleman, as he gazed in amazement on the scene at the end of the long house. "How ragged they are! They must have been hunted through the woods like wild animals. Both of the two in uniform wear jackets of the mounted service, and—stop—as sure as you are born, the taller of the two is a lieutenant of artillery. He has but one shoulder-strap left, and that has too dark a ground for either cavalry or infantry. They may be from the staff. There is something about their uniforms, in spite of rags and dirt, that makes me think so. The other carries a roll of blankets over his shoulder—he must be a soldier; and they have just come in, too, for their haversacks are mighty lean."

It looked as if the poor fellows had found friends at

last; for, while they stood talking with two women at the end of the house, Smith himself, who was a lank mountaineer with a red beard, was lounging by the gate with his gun on his shoulder, as if watching against surprise from the road. Bromley, who had been patiently waiting, now took the glass.

"By Jove!" he cried, "there are four girls there now, and the short officer is going into the house. You are right, Fred; the old man is on guard, with a sharp eye in his head, too. They are all going into the house now, by Neighbor Smith's advice, I fancy. I'll tell you who they are, Fred. They are escaped prisoners from Charleston. They must have been hiding in the woods and swamps for months. If that is the condition of the officers of the United States that were, a thousand times better is our lot on this free mountain-top." And returning the glass, Bromley ventured some bitter reflections on the Congress and the high officials who had conducted the war to a disastrous end.

"We must not lose sight of these unhappy men while they remain in the valley," said Coleman; and, it then being ten o'clock, he settled himself behind the glass, and gave his watch to Bromley, who was to relieve him at twelve.

Philip was too much excited by the presence of the fugitive officers to leave the rocks of his own accord; but Coleman presently sent him to the house for a loaded carbine, which was laid by in a dry niche of granite, to be fired as a signal to the others in case of any movement of importance at the cabin below. For the rest of the morning Smith with his gun kept his post at the gate, and the officers were never once seen outside the cabin. Judging by the volume of smoke from both chimneys, it would appear that they were faring pretty well inside.

Shortly before noon one of the girls ran through the bare woods to the two cottages overlooking the road, and brought back Jones, who relieved Smith at the gate. It was evident that Jones was friendly to the officers, for when he was relieved in turn he went into the house, and it was a long time before he came out.

Whoever was on watch was seldom alone, so keen was the interest of the exiles in the movements of their fellow-soldiers, and in any other happening which might concern them. According to Philip, who took the post of observation at four o'clock, old Shifless bossed the milking from the woodpile as usual. It was plain that he had not been taken into the confidence of the Smiths or the Joneses, and this fact was laid up against him.

After supper all three gathered on the rocky lookout, and remained observing the lights at the cabin of the Smiths long after it was too dark to use the telescope. There were no signs of departure below, and after they returned to the house, chilled by exposure and inaction, they sat until a late hour by the warm fire, discussing the events of the day and laying plans for the morrow.

At the first indication of dawn Bromley dressed and set out for the rocks, while his comrades turned over for another nap, which was taken with one eye open, so excited were they in view of what might happen during the day.

In their drowsy, half-wakeful state it seemed to Coleman and Philip as if no time at all had passed since the departure of Bromley when they were startled by the echoing report of the carbine. Hurrying on their clothing, they scampered across the hard snow to the rocks, where they found Bromley with the telescope fixed on the house of Shifless.

"There the old rogue is," said Bromley, handing the spy-glass to Coleman, "leading his mule out of the stable. He must have got some information during the night, for, after going to the stable with a lantern, he climbed up on to that ridge beyond and looked over at Smith's clearing as if he wanted to satisfy himself that all was quiet there. I suspected he was up to some deviltry as soon as I got out here, for I saw a light in the house, showing first from one window and then from another. Drat his picture!" Bromley continued. "As soon as he began climbing the hill I fired the alarm."

"I never knew him to turn out before eight o'clock," said Philip.

"He certainly means mischief," said Coleman, "for he is saddling the mule. Now he has blown out the lantern and hung it on the bar-post. Now he is mounting, the treacherous old villain! Confound him! there he goes trotting down the road toward the store."

Philip and Bromley took a look at the man, hurrying along in the gray of the morning before another soul was awake in the settlement, and then they saw him turn on to the road which would lead him around the mountain into the Cove.

"If I were only down in his neighborhood now," said Coleman, following Shifless with the telescope, "with a good rifle, I 'd tumble him off that mule. I should be serving my country."

"What country?" sneered Bromley.

To this Coleman made no reply, and the three walked slowly across the mountain to the boulder side. They had not long to wait there before the man on the mule appeared on the road below, and they followed him with scowling eyes until he drew up in front of the Cove post-office, dismounted, and went in.

"Of course," exclaimed Bromley, "the postmaster is a creature of the Confederacy."

In half an hour the two men trotted away together, and soon disappeared among the mountains.

Our heroes turned back, certain in their minds that this stealthy journey of Shifless had been undertaken with hostile intentions toward the three officers who still remained in the cabin under the shadow of Sheep Cliff. They felt keenly their inability to warn them of the danger which hung over them, and hoped that during the day they might see the visitors leaving the valley.

Their anxiety now made it necessary to watch for developments in the Cove as well as in the valley, and they scarcely found time to prepare their meals, which they ate as they moved about. All day the telescope was in transit from one side of the mountain to the other until there was a deep path trodden in the snow. From time to time one or another of the officers was seen near the cabin, and even if they had not been seen at all, the presence of Smith or one of the girls watching at the gate would have been sufficient evidence that the officers were still there. They might be waiting for a guide or the cover of night before going on. The day was unusually cold, and beyond the smoke from the chimneys, and here and there a woman in a doorway, there was no movement in the quiet valley.

Late in the afternoon of this December 24—for it was Christmas eve, and not a very cheerful one on the mountain—Bromley, who was watching on the Cove side, spied a body of men at that very point in the road where the two horsemen had disappeared in the morning. He shouted so lustily for the telescope that both Philip and Coleman joined him with all haste.

What they saw through the glass was a straggling column of mountaineers advancing in single file along the winding road, their steel rifle-barrels catching the last rays of the setting sun. There were thirteen men in the party, of whom about half wore some part of a Confederate uniform; but neither Shifless nor the Cove postmaster was with them. They had scarcely time to pass the glass from one to another, in their excitement, before the men left the road and turned up the mountain-side with a stealthy movement that made it plain they were going into temporary concealment.

A few extracts from Lieutenant Coleman's diary at this point give a vivid picture of what was happening during the night on the mountain and about it.

"I am writing by the light of the fire in our house on this Christmas eve, at 10:30 o'clock by my watch, powerless to warn our friends at the cabin of the impending calamity. Soon after dark, fire appeared on mountain-side, and it is now burning brightly, as reported by Philip, who has just returned to the lookout.

"12, midnight. Have just come in—fire still visible.

"12:35. Philip reports that fire has just been extinguished on mountain-side. Sparks indicated fire was put out by beating and scattering the brands. We are all about to go to Point of Rocks—shall probably be up all night."

It seems that as soon as day began to dawn faintly on the mountain-tops, and while it was still dark in the valley, the three soldiers were crouching on the rocks eagerly awaiting light in the clearing. First the whitewashed walls of the cabin came into view, and then, in the gray dawn, as they fully expected, they began to distinguish motionless figures stationed at regular intervals in the clearing, and forming an armed cordon about the house. There was no sign of smoke from the stone chimneys, nor any other evidence that the inmates had been disturbed by the soldiers or had awakened of their own accord.

There was one hope left. The officers might have gone away during the night. They should soon know; and meanwhile the snowy mountains reared their dark ridges against the slowly reddening eastern sky, and a great silence lay on the valley.

CHAPTER XI

IN WHICH THE SOLDIERS MAKE A MAP

THE forbearance of the captors to disturb their prisoners was puzzling to the three soldiers huddled together on the point of rocks. Through the telescope the men could now be plainly seen, in their rough mountain dress, moving to and fro on their stations, and apparently keeping under cover where trees or outhouses were available as a mask. At one point several men were grouped together behind a fodder-stack, as if in consultation, and on the road could be seen one who seemed to be watching impatiently for some expected arrival.

Holding the telescope soon grew tiresome, and they passed it from one to another, that no movement in the gruesome pantomime might escape their observation; and the observer for the time being broke the silence at intervals with details of what he saw.

"There!" cried Philip, at last, "the men are getting lively behind the fodder-stack. Now the fellow in the road is waving his hat. Hold on! There comes a man—

IN WHICH THE SOLDIERS MAKE A MAP

two men—on horseback. Now the sentinels are moving in toward the cabin."

Thus the cordon was drawn close about the house, in which the inmates still showed no signs of life. The horsemen dismounted and tied their horses to the fence, and then, with an armed guard, advanced to the door. Lieutenant Coleman looked at his watch. It was twenty minutes after seven. At seven twenty-eight the old mountaineer appeared, and was passed down the line to the road. Next came the three officers, one after the other, and they were removed to one side under guard. Then the four women seemed to be driven out of the house by the soldiers, and forced along by violence into the road. Some of the men appeared to be breaking the windows of the cabin, and others were running out of the open door, appropriating some objects and ruthlessly destroying others. For the first time the soldier exiles realized how far they were removed, by their own will, from a world in which they had no part. The sufferers were their friends whom they knew not, and to help whom they had no power. They were like spirits looking down from a world above on the passions of mortals—as helpless to interfere as the motionless rocks.

After a brief consultation the mounted men rode away to the north, while the prisoners, with their guards, advanced in the opposite direction and soon disappeared behind that ridge up which Shifless had climbed to look over in the gray of the morning of the day before. A puff of smoke burst from the deserted cabin and rose like a tower into the frosty air. Fire gleamed through the broken windows, and red tongues of flame licked about the dry logs, and lashed and forked under the eaves and about the edges of the shingled roof. The reflection from the flames reddened the snow in the little clearing. The stacks caught fire. The boughs of the orchard withered and crisped in the fierce heat.

Now, as if satisfied with their work of destruction, the men who had remained at the house joined the others behind the ridge, and the armed guards, with their miserable prisoners, soon reappeared, moving over the snow under the bare trees. The three soldiers lay out on the rocks above to watch the poor captives picking their way down a stony, winding trail, forming one straggling file between two flanking columns of mountaineers. Knowing something of the stoical ways of these people, they could feel the silence of that gloomy progress. They even fancied they could hear the crunching of the snow, the rolling of displaced stones on the frosty hillside, the crackling of brittle twigs under foot, and the subdued sobbing of the women.

Steadily the procession of ill omen moved along over the snow under the thin trees, disappearing and reappearing and dwindling in the distance, until it was lost behind the spurs of the mountain called Chimney Top. By this time the roof of the house had fallen into the burning mass between the two stone chimneys; the sun had risen, and the dense column of smoke cast a writhing shadow against the snowy face of Sheep Cliff.

"THE FOWLS HUNG ABOUT THE DOOR."

When the glass was brought to bear on the house and road below, it revealed Shifless and the Cove postmaster riding quietly home on their mules, doubtless well satisfied with the evil deed their heads had planned.

As the three soldiers turned back in the direction of their house, Bromley was in a rage, and Philip could no longer command himself. All three were worn and haggard with loss of sleep, and depressed by the outcome of the affair in the valley.

In fact, the disheartening effect of the experiences connected with this first Christmas continued to oppress our exiles well into the next year. If, in the narrow valley on which they were privileged to look down, three officers of the old armies had been thus hunted and dragged off before their eyes, they had reason to believe that fragments of those armies were receiving similar or worse treatment wherever they might be found. Time and their daily work gradually calmed their minds and helped them to forget the pain of what they had seen. They missed the company of the bear, too; for even before this great disturbance of their tranquillity that amusing companion of their solitude had burrowed himself away, to consume his own fat, where not even their telescope could discover him for several months.

Presently the winter snows became deeper on the mountain, and they were confined more and more to the house. The Slow-John was frozen up in the branch, and the fowls, which could no longer forage for their own living, hung about the door for the scraps from the table and an occasional handful of corn. They roosted in the cabin of the old man of the mountain, and now and then, in return for their keep, laid an egg, which was often frozen before it was found.

The soft, clean husks of the corn, added to the pine boughs, made comfortable beds, and the tents spread over the blankets provided abundant covering. Great bunches of catnip and pennyroyal for tea hung from the rafters, and even the wild gentian, potent to cure all ailments, was not forgotten in the winter outfit.

The prayer-book and Army Regulations, which formed their library, were read and re-read, and discussed until theology and the art of clothing and feeding an army were worn threadbare. Philip, who was blessed with a vivid imagination and great originality, made up the most marvelous ghost-stories and the most heartrending and finally soul-satisfying romances, which were recited in the evenings before the fire, to the huge enjoyment of his companions. If it was romance, a fat pine-knot thrust between the logs illumined the interior and searched the farthest corners and crannies of the room with a flood of light; and in case it was a ghost-story, the logs were left to burn low and fall piecemeal into the red coals before the eyes of the three figures sitting half revealed in sympathetic obscurity.

One of the most interesting incidents of the first winter was the construction, by Lieutenant Coleman, of a map of the "old United States," and the plotting thereon of the Confederacy as they supposed it to be. When it is remembered that the map was drawn entirely from memory, the clear topographical knowledge of the officer was, to say the least, surprising.

The first reference to the map is found in Lieutenant Coleman's entry in the diary for the 24th of January, 1865:

"As we were sitting before the fire last night, George introduced a subject which, by common consent, we have rather avoided any reference to or conversation upon. This related to the probable boundaries of the new nation established by the triumphant Confederates. We had no doubt that the Confederacy embraced all the States which were slaveholding States at the outbreak of the Rebellion; and as they doubtless had made Washington their capital, it was more than probable that they had added little Delaware to Maryland on their northern border. We assumed that so long as there were two governments in the old territory, the Ohio River would be accepted as a natural boundary as far as to the Mississippi; but we were of widely different opinions as to the line of separation thence.

"George, who is inclined to the darker view, is of the opinion that the Southern republic, if it be a republic at all, would certainly demand an opening to the Pacific Ocean, and therefore must embrace a part, if not the whole, of California.

"February 16. We have been confined to the house two days by a driving snow-storm, and the territorial extent of the Confederacy has come up again, not, however, for the first time since the discussion on the 23d of January. As we still have one stormy month before the opening of spring, I have determined to enter upon the construction of a map which shall lay down the probable boundaries of the two nations. When George and I are unable to agree, the point in dispute will be argued before Philip, and settled by the votes of the three."

On February 17, then, this map was begun on the inner side of one of the rubber ponchos after buttoning down and gluing with pitch the opening in the center. It was stretched on a frame, and thus provided a clean white canvas five feet square on which to draw the map.

If Lieutenant Coleman and his companions had known that General Sherman, after whom they had named their island in the sky and whom they mourned as dead, was that very morning marching into the city of Columbia, the capital of South Carolina, with all his bands playing and flags flying, the map would never have been made, and the life on the mountain would have come to a sudden end. Fortunately for the continuance of this history, they were ignorant of that fact, and Lieutenant Coleman on this very day began plotting his map with charcoal. After going over the coasts and watercourses and establishing the boundaries of States, and that greatest and most difficult of all boundaries, the one between "the two countries," he would blow off the charcoal and complete the details with ink. Of this necessary fluid there was a canteen full, which had been made in the fall from oak-galls (lumps or balls produced on the oak-leaves by tiny insects) and the purple pokeberries which had been gathered from the field below the ledge. The oak-leaves had been steeped in warm water, and this mixture, together with the berries, had been strained through a cloth and bottled up in the canteen.

While at West Point, Cadet Coleman, of the class of '63, had devoted himself to mapping, and he believed he was tolerably familiar with his subject until, at the very outset, difficulties began to arise. He found that his knowledge about the Northwestern Territories was shaky, and it was difficult to convince Bromley that Arkansas was not west of Kansas.

They finally gave little Delaware to the Confederacy, accepting the bay and river as a natural geographical separation. Thence they followed the southern boundary of Pennsylvania to the Ohio River, the Ohio and Mississippi to the southern boundary of Iowa, and thence west and south on the northern and western frontiers of Missouri. The Indian Territory became the first point of disagreement.

Under date of March 1, 1865, Lieutenant Coleman says:

"With the aid of Philip, I pressed the boundary line south to the Red River. We all conceded Texas to the Confederacy. I was disposed to establish the extreme western boundary of the Confederacy as identical with the western frontier of Texas. George allowed this so far as the Rio Grande formed a natural boundary along the frontier of Mexico, but stoutly insisted that the successful Southerners would never consent to a settlement which did not extend their borders to the Pacific Ocean. To this claim on the part of the South he contended that the imbecility of Congress and the timidity of Northern leaders would offer little or no opposition. He held that if they took part of California, they might as well take the whole; and in either case they would take New Mexico and Arizona as the natural connection with their Pacific territory.

"I contended that California had never been a slave State, and would never consent to such an arrangement. To this George replied that California was without troops, and that her wishes would not be a factor in the solution of the problem; that the South, flushed with victory, could not be logically expected to content itself with less; that it would be a matter to be settled between the two governments, and that, for his part, he saw no reason to believe that the North, in view of its blunders civil and its failures military, would have the power or the courage to prevent such seizure by the enemy. Philip leaned to this view, and was even willing to throw in Utah for sentimental reasons."

Bromley showed great skill and cleverness in advocating his peculiar views. When he had a point to gain, with the natural cunning of a legal mind, he took care to begin his argument by claiming much more than he expected to establish. Thus, not content with the concession of California and the southern tier of Territories leading

"PHILIP MADE UP THE MOST MARVELOUS STORIES, WHICH WERE RECITED BEFORE THE FIRE."

thereto, he called the attention of the others to the great Rocky Mountain range, offering itself, from the northwestern extremity of Texas to the British possessions, as a natural geographical wall between nations. He admitted that the Western men had been the bone and sinew of the late fruitless struggle; but they were the hardy soldiers of Illinois, Wisconsin, Iowa, and Kansas, still far to the east of the great mountain-range, with vast uncivilized Territories between.

To this view Lieutenant Coleman opposed the jealousy of the great ally of the South as not likely to favor an unequal partition; he said that England would certainly not lend her aid to bringing the more aggressive of the two nations up to her own colonial borders. Besides, he contended, the South was without a navy, and at the outset could never defend such a great addition to her already vastly superior coast-line.

This long argument resulted in a compromise, and by the decision of Philip, California, Arizona, and New Mexico were given to the Confederacy, and half the Pacific coast was saved to the old government.

Bromley's matter-of-fact character had no sentimental side. He was a worker, and no dreamer. He threw himself with all the weight of his convictions and the force of his well-trained mind into the discussion of the extent of the Confederate victory; but the moment the boundary was settled he seemed to forget the existence of the map and to lose himself in the next piece of work.

After completing the outlines of the map in ink, Lieutenant Coleman began laying a tone of lines over the whole Confederacy. As the work progressed, the three soldiers watched the new power creeping like an ominous shadow over the map. The one break in the expanse of gloom was the white star at the northwestern corner of North Carolina, which marked the location of Sherman Territory. When the map was finished and hung on the logs, the Confederacy looked like nothing so much as a huge dragon crouching on the Gulf of Mexico, with the neck and head elevated along the Pacific and the tail brushing Cuba.

Although they accepted the map without further discussion, its white face, looking down on them from the wall as they sat about the evening fire, provoked many a talk about affairs in the world below. The time for the election of a new President had passed since they had been on the mountain. After the complete and pitiful collapse of Lincoln's administration, they had no doubt that McClellan had been elected. Philip thought the new capital should be located at Piqua, Ohio (which was where his uncle lived), as it was near the center of population!

But Bromley favored the city of Cleveland. Ohio, he pointed out, extended entirely across the Union, and, as the State which linked the two parts together, it would need to be strongly guarded, and the capital with its troops and fortifications would strengthen that weak link in the chain. Cincinnati was too close to the enemy's territory to be thought of as a capital.

Shortly before undertaking the map, Lieutenant Coleman had the good fortune to bring down a large gray

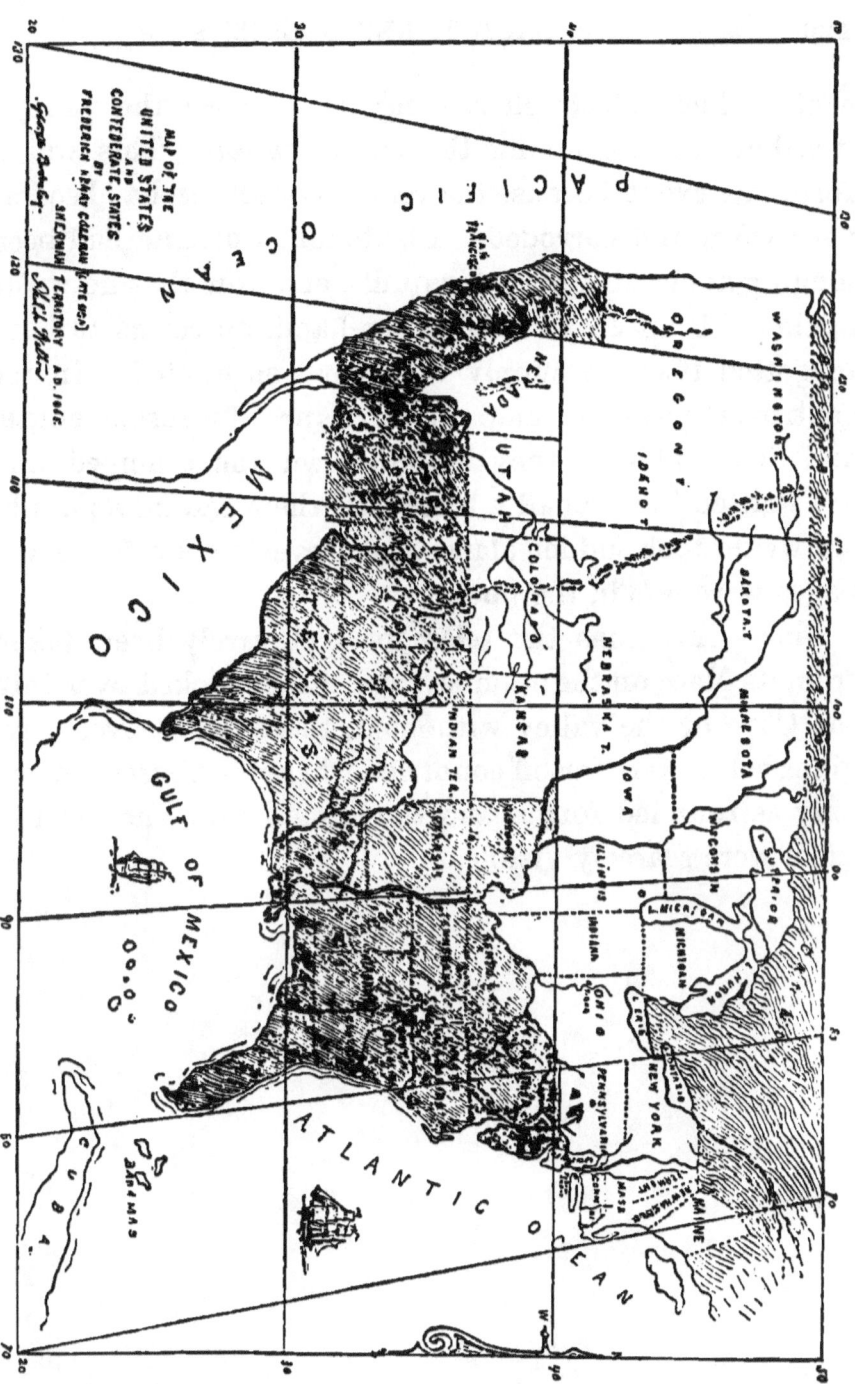

eagle, which, although soaring high above the valleys, was but just skimming the mountain-top. This was a fortunate event, because the very last steel pen had become very worn and corroded. Lieutenant Coleman had been longing above all things for quills, and now that he wrote again with an easy and flowing hand, he seems to have forgotten that his supply of paper was limited. In the controversy over the map the entries are of unusual length, and then suddenly they become brief and cramped, and are written in so small a hand that there can be no doubt the writer took sudden alarm on discovering how few blank pages were left in the book.

Since Christmas the telescope had rarely been taken from its place on the chimney, and if they looked over into the Cove or the valley without it, those snow-covered regions below were far-off countries, where the houses showed only as rounded forms, and the human ants who lived in them were scarcely visible.

CHAPTER XII

HOW THE BEAR DISGRACED HIMSELF

AT last the long winter came to an end. By the middle of March the warm sun and soft south winds began to thaw the February snows. On such a day, when the afternoon sun beat with unusual warmth on the northern face of the mountain, the three soldiers stood together in front of the house, noting everywhere the joyful signs of the approach of spring. The snow, where it lay thickest in the hollows of the plateau, was soft and porous and grimy with dirt. There were bare spaces here and there on the ground, and where a stick or a stone showed through the thin crust the snow had retired around it as if it gave out a heat of its own. The melting icicles pendent from the eaves glittered in the sun and dripped into the channels alongside the walls.

They had a great longing to see the grass and the leaves again and welcome the early birds of spring. As they looked about on these hopeful signs in the midst of the great stillness to which they had become used, a sudden deafening crash rang in their startled ears. The sound was like the explosion of a mine or the dull roar of a siege-mortar at a little distance away. It came from the Cove to the north, and the first crash was followed by lesser reports, and each sound was echoed back from the mountains beyond.

The first thought of the three soldiers was of the opening of a battle. Their first fear was that a great mass of earth and rock had fallen from the edge of the plateau to the base of the mountain. They made their way cautiously in the direction of the sound, almost distrusting the ground under their feet. The gnarled chestnuts on the edge of the cliff were as firmly rooted as ever. When they had advanced to where Philip's sharp eyes caught the first view of the postmaster's cabin through the twisted tree-trunks, he remembered the words of Andy, the guide, on the night when they had waited for the moon to go down. He quickly caught the arms of his companions.

"It's the avalanche," he said — "the icicles and the ice falling into the Cove from the face of the great boulder."

They could see tiny figures standing about the cabin, and they shrank back lest they, too, might be seen by the people, who were evidently gazing with all their eyes at the top of the mountain.

Just then there was another deafening crash, and at intervals all day long they heard the falling of the ice.

"They are the opening guns of spring," said Lieutenant Coleman; and now that they knew what the sound was, they listened eagerly for each report.

Late on that very afternoon, as they sat together outside the house, they saw Tumbler, the bear, shambling down the hillside in front of the house, and they had no doubt he had been awakened from his winter's nap by the roar of the avalanche. He was thin of flesh and ragged of fur, and so weak on his clumsy legs that he sat down at short intervals to rest. He made his way first to the branch, where he refreshed himself with a drink, and then came on with renewed vigor toward the house. He was such a very disreputable-looking bear, and had been gone so long, and must be so dangerously hungry, that the men stood up doubtfully at his approach until they saw a weak movement of his stumpy tail and the mild look in his brown eyes as he seated himself on the chips and lolled out his red tongue.

Philip brought him a handful of roast potatoes, which he devoured with a relish, and then stood up so handsomely to ask for more that they rolled him raw ones until his hunger was satisfied, after which he waddled through the open door, and lay down for another nap in his old place by the fire, just as if he had gone out but yesterday, which was probably just what he thought he had done.

By this time the last page of the station journal had been used, and Lieutenant Coleman had added to it the five fly-leaves of the precious Blue Book, which he had cut out neatly with his knife. Paper was so scarce at last that on this March 16, which was the day the bear woke up, the circumstance of the avalanche alone was recorded, and that was entered after the date in the most wonderfully small and cramped letters you can imagine. Now, Philip was of the opinion that the return of the bear was of quite as much importance as the falling of the ice. It happened that he had in his breast pocket a letter which had been written to him by his uncle. It was postmarked, "Piqua, Ohio," and addressed, "Philip Welton, Co. C, 2d Ohio Infy., Camp near Resaca, Ga." Philip had been looking over Coleman's shoulder as he made the cramped entry in the diary.

"Now look here," said he, taking up the quill as it was laid down; "if you don't choose to make a record of the bear, I will." So taking from his pocket the letter, he wrote across the top of the envelop:

"WHITESIDE MOUNTAIN, March 16, 1865.
"Tumbler, the bear, woke up to-day.
"(Signed) PHILIP WELTON,
"GEORGE BROMLEY,
"FREDERICK HENRY COLEMAN."

"Well," said Coleman, "what are you going to do with that? Drop it over into the Cove?"

"Not a bit of it," said Philip. "I am just going to keep the record out of respect to the bear"; and with that, as it happened, he put the envelop back in one pocket and the letter in another. But a few weeks later, when the snow had quite gone and the buds were beginning to swell on the trees, Philip was chopping on the hill where the boulder side of the mountain joined the cliff above the spring; and as he grew warm with his work he cast off his cavalry jacket, and it happened in some way that the envelop on which he had written fell out into the grass. Philip did not notice this loss at the time, and it was a week before he missed the envelop. He kept his loss to himself at first, but as he became alarmed lest it should blow over into the Cove and disclose their hiding-place, he confessed to Lieutenant Coleman what had happened.

The three soldiers searched everywhere for this dangerous paper, except in the snug place under the tuft of grass where it lay. It was suspected that Philip was repenting of the agreement he had made to remain on the mountain, and both Coleman and Bromley lectured him roundly for his carelessness. While Philip was still chafing under the suspicions of his comrades, all the more that he was conscious of his perfect loyalty to the old flag and to the compact they had made together for its sake, the bear was growing stronger every day and more mischievous. Although he had the whole plateau to roam over, nothing seemed to please Tumbler so much as to nose about and dig into the grave of the old man of the mountain. He was such a wicked bear that the more they kicked and cuffed him away, the more stubbornly he came back to his unholy work; and then it appeared that the light soil of the mound had been taken possession of by a colony of ants. It was a temptation such as no hungry bear could resist, and the sacrilege was so offensive to the three soldiers that they resolved to remove the last remnant of the ant-hill and fill it in with clay in which no insect could live. It was after supper when they came to this resolution, and they fell to work at once with the wooden spade and a piece of tent-cloth, in which Philip carried the dirt a stone's-throw away and piled it into a new mound. The bear seemed to think this was all for his benefit, and while the work went merrily on he rooted into the new heap and wagged his stumpy tail with every evidence of gratitude and satisfaction.

It was a sufficiently disagreeable task for Coleman and Bromley, whose legs and bodies were bitten by the ants until they danced with pain. At the same time the little pests went up Philip's sleeves and came out on his neck. Bad as the business was, they set their teeth and kept at work, determined to finish it now they had begun. Of course the colony was mostly near the surface of the ground; but when they had gone down three feet into the sandy soil there were still ants burrowing about.

Now, Bromley was a man of great resolution and perseverance, and although it was growing dark he had no thought of stopping work; so he called for a pine torch, which Coleman held on the bank above. When the earth gave way, the oak slab with the peculiar inscription, "One who wishes to be forgotten," was tenderly removed and leaned against the hut, to be reverently reset the next day. Annoying as the ants were, the soldiers continued their work with that feeling of awe which always attends the disturbing of a grave; and as they dug they spoke with charity and tenderness of the old man of the mountain. It made them think of the time when they themselves would be laid to rest in the same soil; and if they breathed any inward prayer, it was that their remains might sleep undisturbed. Although they were young, and death seemed a long way off, the thought came to them of the last survivor, and how lonely he would be, and how, when he should die, there would be no one left to bury his poor body in the ground.

"Whatever happens," said Philip, "I don't want to be the last."

The pine torch flared and smoked in the cool night wind, and lighted the solemn faces of the three soldiers as well as the hole in the earth, where Bromley still stood to his middle. There was yet a little loose earth to be thrown out before they left the work for the night, and Philip had brought some sticks of wood to lay over the grave lest in the morning the bear should begin to dig where they had left off. He had, in fact, come up and seated himself in the circle of light, and was looking on with great interest at their proceedings.

"I declare," said Bromley, just then, straightening himself, "I have gone too far already. My spade struck on the coffin—that is, I think it did. Perhaps I had better see what condition it is in. What do you think, Fred?"

"No," said Philip; "cover it up."

"It will be as well," said Lieutenant Coleman, "now that we have the opportunity, to see that everything is all right. I can't help feeling that the old man's remains are in our care."

"Hold the light nearer, then," said Bromley, as he got

down on his knees and commenced to paw away the loose earth with his hands.

Philip was silent, and, soldier though he was, his face blanched in the neighborhood of one poor coffin.

Both the men outside were staring intently into the open grave. The torch-light fell broadly on Bromley's back, and cast a black shadow from his bent body into the space below, where his hands were at work.

"Well, this is queer!" said he, straightening his back and showing a surprised face to the light. "I've struck the chime of a cask."

"No!" cried Coleman and Philip together.

"Yes, I have," said Bromley. "Hand me the spade."

Now the work of digging was begun in good earnest, and, I am afraid, with less awe than before of what lay below. Light as the soil was, the opening had to be enlarged, and it was hard upon midnight when the small beer-keg was free enough to be moved from its resting-place. With the first joggle Bromley gave it, there was a sound of chinking like coin.

"Do you hear that?" exclaimed Bromley. "That's not the sound of bones."

"It's money!" cried Philip.

Lieutenant Coleman said nothing, but jumping down to the aid of Bromley, they lifted it out on the grass, where it rolled gently down a little slope, chink-a-ty-chink, chink-a-ty-chink.

"Bring the ax!"

"No; let's roll it into the house!"

"It's money!"

"It's nails!"

"Bring it in to the fire," said Lieutenant Coleman, going ahead with the torch. So they rolled the tough old cask, chink-a-ty-chink, around the cabin and up to the house, into the open door and across the earthen floor, and set it on end on the stone hearth. They were reeking with perspiration. Coleman threw the torch upon the smoldering logs, and by the time Bromley had the ax there was a ruddy light through the room.

"Stand back," he cried as he swung the ax aloft.

Three times the ax rang on the head of the cask, the firelight glittering in the eyes of the soldiers, before the strong head gave way on one side, and three golden guineas bounced out on to the hearth. Bromley dropped the ax, and then all three, without deigning to notice the gold pieces upon the floor, thrust their hands deep down into the shining mass of gold coin.

All hustled and pushed one another at the opening. Philip was on the point of striking out right and left in sheer excitement; and in their scramble the cask was overturned so that the yellow pieces poured out upon the floor and the hearth, and some flopped into the fire, while others rolled here and there into the dark corners of the room. The golden guineas which first appeared were now covered with gold double-eagles, and there were a few silver coins in the bottom of the cask.

The three soldiers hugged one another with delight.

"We are rich!" cried Philip.

"Let's count our treasure," said Coleman. "The double-eagles first—fifty to a thousand."

Forgotten was the old man of the mountain, forgotten were their weariness and the lateness of the hour, as they eagerly fell a-counting.

They piled the shining yellow columns on the mantelpiece; and when that was full, without stopping to count the thousands, they began bunches of piles on the hard floor.

They could hardly believe that such a treasure had fallen to their possession.

In their greedy delight they utterly forgot the old flag of the thirty-five stars, and the total defeat of the Union armies, as they toiled and counted.

Philip was the first to yield to the demands of tired nature. With his hands full of gold, he sank down on his bunk and fell asleep. Lieutenant Coleman was the next; and as the cock began to crow at earliest dawn, Bromley bolted the door for the first time since the house had been built, and crept exhausted into his blankets.

The treasure was found, as shown by the diary, on Friday, April 14, in the year 1865, on the very night of the murder of the good President whom the three soldiers believed to be living somewhere, a monument of failure and incapacity.

The entry was in a few brief words, and by the Sunday which followed, Lieutenant Coleman would not have exchanged the four blank leaves of the diary for the whole treasure they had dug up. After the first excitement

"THE CASK WAS OVERTURNED SO THAT THE YELLOW PIECES POURED OUT UPON THE FLOOR."

of their discovery they began to realize that the yellow stamped pieces were of no value except as a medium of exchange, and that, as there was nothing on the mountain for which to exchange them, they were of no value at all. If they had found a saucepan or a sack of coffee in the cask, they would have had some reason to rejoice.

So it fell out that within a week's time the gold was looked upon as so much lumber, and the cask which held it was kicked into a dark corner, neglected and despised. Some of the coins were even trodden under foot, and others lay among the chips at the door.

On the evening of the second Sunday after the discovery of the gold, they sat together outside the door of the house, and tried to think of some likely thing the cask might have held more useless than the guineas and double-eagles; and, hard as they tried, they could name nothing more worthless. The result was that they turned away to their beds, feeling poor and dissatisfied, and down on their luck.

Now it happened, as the three soldiers lay asleep in their bunks that night, and while Tumbler slept too, with his nose and his hairy paws in the light, cool ashes of the fireplace (for the nights were warm now), there came up a brisk wind which blew across the mountain from the southwest. This rising wind went whistling on its way, tossing the tree-tops, up on the hill above the birches, whirling the dry leaves across the plateau, scattering them on the field below the ledge, and even dropping some stragglers away down into the Cove far below.

At first this wind only shook the tuft of grass that overhung the lost envelop, and then, as it grew stronger, whirled it from its snug hiding-place, and tumbled it over and over among the dry chestnut-burs and the old, gray, dead limbs.

If the envelop came to a rest, this wind was never content to leave its plaything alone for long. When it landed the little paper against a stump and held it fluttering there until that particular gust was out of breath, the envelop fell to the ground of its own weight, only to be picked up again and tossed on, little by little, always in the same direction, until at last it lay exposed on the brow of the hill to a braver and stronger blast, which lifted it high into the air and sent it sailing over the roof of the house.

This envelop, with the names of the three soldiers and their hiding-place written out in a fair, round hand, might have sailed along on the southwest wind until it fell at the door of the post-office in the Cove but for the queer way it had of navigating the air. It would turn over and over on its way, or shoot up, or dart to one side, or take some unexpected course; and so just as it was sailing smoothly above the house, its sharp edge turned in the wind, and with a backward dive it struck hard on the rock below Philip's leach. Just a breath of wind turned it over and over on the stone, until it fell noiselessly into the pool of lye.

Now, Lieutenant Coleman chanced to come out first in the morning; and when he saw the lost envelop floating on the dark-brown pool alongside a hen's egg, which had been placed there to test the strength of the liquid, he was glad it had blown no farther. The paper had turned very yellow in the strong potash, and so he fished it out with a twig, and carried it across to the branch by the Slow-John, and dipped it into the water. When he picked it out it was still slimy to the touch, and the letters had faded a little. He brushed a word with his finger, and the letters dissolved under his eyes.

He gave a great cry of joy; for in that instant he saw the possibility of converting into blank paper, for keeping their records, the five hundred and ninety-four pages of the Revised Army Regulations of 1863.

CHAPTER XIII

HOW THE BEAR DISTINGUISHED HIMSELF

IF the old man of the mountain was not in his grave, where was he? He had certainly not gone back to the world and left the buried treasure behind him. If the grave had been empty, the soldiers might have suspected foul play. Josiah Woodring, who had been his agent and provider, had already been five years in his own grave at the time they had arrived on the mountain. As long as they believed that the bones of the old man were quietly at rest under the oak slab in the garden spot, the condition of the hut, neglected and going to decay, was sufficient evidence that he had died there, and that no one had occupied it for more than five years before. With almost his last breath Josiah had announced his death to the doctor from the settlement; and under such solemn circumstances it was impossible to believe that he had stated anything but the truth. He had not mentioned, it is true, the precise time when the old man died.

After the night when the treasure was found, the three

soldiers, to thoroughly satisfy themselves, had cleared away the earth down to the bed-rock. Indeed, the cask itself was evidence enough that the bones of the old man were not below it, for he himself must have buried that. If Josiah had known of its existence, it would certainly have traveled down through the settlement in his two-steer cart, like any other honest cask, and neither cattle nor driver would have ever come back. After taking such a load to market, Josiah would have established himself in luxury in his ignorant way, and probably cut a great splurge in the "low country," with no end of pomp and vulgarity.

The three soldiers studied this problem with much care, weighing all the evidence for and against. They even hit upon a plan of determining when the old man came limping through the settlement of Cashiers behind Josiah's cart, covered with dust, and staggering under the weight of his leathern knapsack. They emptied out the little keg of gold on the earthen floor a second time, and began a search for the latest date on the coins. Some were remarkably old and badly worn. A few of the guinea pieces bore the heads of the old Georges and "Dei gratia Rex," and 17— this and 17— that, and some of the figures were as smooth as the pate, and as blind as the eyes, of the king on the coin. The newest double-eagles—and there were quite a number of them—bore the date 1833, so it must have been in that year or the year following that the old man without a name had given up the world and become a hermit on the mountain.

They decided that he must have had his own ideas about the vanity of riches, and that after doling out his gold, or, more likely, his small silver pieces, with exceeding stinginess to Josiah for the small services rendered him, when he saw his end approaching, he had buried the cask of treasure, and set up the slab above it, trusting to the superstition with which the mountain people regarded the desecration of a grave to protect the gold for all time. It would certainly have protected it from any examination by the soldiers but for the strange behavior of the bear, who had no delicate scruples. The old man had probably told Josiah, with a cunning leer in his eyes, that the empty grave was a blind to deceive any one who might climb to the top of the mountain, as the hunters had done long before, and very likely he had given him a great big silver half-dollar to wink at this little plan. When death did really come at last to claim its own, it was evident that Josiah, faithful to the old man's request, had either taken his remains down the mountain or buried them somewhere on the plateau without mound or slab to reveal the place, and, as likely as not, he had found enough small change in the old miser's pockets to pay him for his trouble.

Thus the mystery of the old man of the mountain was settled by the three soldiers, after much discussion, and the cask of gold was trundled back into the dark corner of the house, where they threw their waste, and such guineas and double-eagles as had joggled out upon the floor were kicked after it.

Directly after the lost envelop had turned up in the

pool of lye, Lieutenant Coleman had made his arrangements for the manufacture of blank paper for the diary. The Blue Book was his personal property, but before commencing its destruction he counseled with Bromley, who, as a man of letters, he felt, under the circumstances, had an equal interest with himself in the fate of one half of their common library. Bromley, seated on the bank alongside the leach, was engaged at the time in making a birch broom, and as he threw down the bunch of twigs a shade of disappointment overspread his handsome face. He said that he had never thoroughly appreciated the work of the learned board of compilers until his present exile, and that it contained flights of eloquence and scraps of poetry—if you read between the lines.

"But, putting all joking aside," said Bromley, "begin with a single leaf by way of experiment, and let us see first what will be the effect on the fiber of the paper; and then, if everything works well, we will first sacrifice the index and the extracts from the Acts of that renegade Congress whose imbecility has blotted a great nation from the map of the world."

Lieutenant Coleman had more confidence in the result of the experiment they were about to make than had Bromley, for the increased length of his entry in the diary shows that he was no longer economizing paper:

"April 26, 1865. Wednesday. We have cut out ten leaves of the index of the Blue Book, which we scattered loosely on the surface of the lye in the cavity of the rock.

After twenty minutes I removed a leaf which had undergone no perceptible change in appearance, and washed it thoroughly in running water. While so doing I was pleased to find that with the lightest touch of my fingers the ink dissolved, leaving underneath only a faint trace of the letters, which would in no way interfere with my writing. It required much patience to cleanse the paper of the slimy deposit of potash.

"Thursday, April 27, 1865. Of the leaves prepared yesterday, two, which were less carefully washed than the others, are somewhat yellowed by the potash and show signs of brittleness.

"April 30. We have continued our paper-making experiments, and find that a longer bath in a weaker solution of lye has the same effect on the ink, and is less injurious to the fiber of the paper. Philip has burned a lot of holes in one of the cracker-boxes, in which we place the leaves, leaving them to soak in the running water."

Thus it turned out that the dangerous envelop, by a freak of the sportive wind, was made to play an important part in the economy of the exiles, while the cask of gold stood neglected in the corner, and the summer of 1865 began with no lack of paper on which to record its events. Both Philip and the bear had been in temporary disgrace, the one for losing the tell-tale envelop, and the other for disturbing the sacred quiet of a grave. Both cases of misbehavior had resulted in important discoveries, but the mishap of Philip had produced such superior benefits that the bear was fairly distanced in the race. This may have been the reason that prompted Tumbler to try his hand, or rather his paw, again, for he was a much cleverer bear than you would think to look at his small eyes and flat skull. At any rate, one hot morning in July he put his foot in it once more, and very handsomely, too, for the benefit of his masters.

It was Philip who caught the first view of him well up on the trunk of the tallest chestnut on the plateau, which, growing in a sheltered place under the northwest hill, had not been dwarfed and twisted by the winds like its fellows higher up. At the moment he was discovered, he was licking his paw in the most peaceful and contented way, while the air about his head was thick with a small cloud of angry bees, darting furiously among the limbs and thrusting their hot stings into his shaggy coat, seeming to disturb him no more than one small gnat can disturb an ox. The soldiers had been deprived of sweets since the last of the sugar had been used, in the early winter, and a supply of honey would just fit the cravings of their educated taste. Share and share alike, bear and man, was the unwritten law of Sherman Territory, and so, while Philip shouted for the ax, he began to throw clubs at Tumbler, which were so much larger and more persuasive than the stings of the bees that the bear began promptly to back his way down the trunk of the tree.

Coleman and Bromley appeared in a jiffy, casting off their jackets and rolling up their sleeves as they came.

When the chips began to fly, Tumbler sat down to watch, evidently feeling that some superior intelligence was at work for his benefit, while the stupid bees kept swarming about the hole above, except a few stray ones who had not yet got tired of burrowing into the shaggy coat of the bear, and these now turned their attention to the men and were promptly knocked down by wisps of grass in the hands of Coleman and Philip, while Bromley plied the ax. If only they had had a supply of sulphur, by waiting until the bees were settled at night, they could have burned some in the opening made by the ax, and with the noxious fumes destroyed the last bee in the tree. Then, too, if they had been in less of a hurry they might have waited until a frosty morning in November had benumbed the bees; but in that case Tumbler would have eaten all the honey he could reach with his paws.

As it was, the swarm extended so low that, as soon as the ax opened the first view into the hollow trunk, the bees began to appear, and the opening had to be stuffed with grass, and a bucket of water which Philip brought did not come amiss before the chopping was done. All this time Tumbler licked his jaws, and kept his beady eyes fixed on the top of the tree, like a good coon dog, and never stirred his stumps until, with the last blow of the ax, the old tree creaked, and swayed at the top, and fell with a great crash down the hill.

The three soldiers ran off to a safe distance as soon as the tree began to fall, while Tumbler, after regarding their flight with a look of disgust, walked deliberately into

"THEY DROVE HIM OFF WITH STICKS AND STONES."

the thick of the battle, and began to crunch the dripping comb as coolly as a pig eats corn. The brittle trunk of the old tree had split open as it fell, and for twenty feet of its length the mass of yellow honey lay exposed to the gaze of the men, while the infuriated bees darkened the air above it, and made a misty halo about the head of the happy bear.

The happiness of Tumbler was not altogether uninterrupted, for the soldiers drove him off now and again with sticks and stones; but however far he retired from the tree, he was surrounded and defended by such an army of bees that it was quite out of the question to capture him. There was no end of the honey; but the worst of it was, the bear was eating the whitest and newest of the combs, and when at last his greedy appetite was satisfied, and he came of his own accord to the house, he brought such disagreeable company with him that the soldiers got out through the door and windows as best they could, leaving him in undisputed possession—very much as his lamented mother had held the fort on that night when her little cub, Tumbler, had slept in the ashes the year before.

There was nothing else to be done but to walk about for the rest of the day; for until nightfall there was a line of bees from the house to the tree. The soldiers secured the bear by closing the door and windows, but it was not yet clear how they could obtain the honey. Coleman and Bromley were city-bred, but Philip had been brought up in the country, and he had received some other things from his uncle besides kicks and cuffs and a knowledge of how to run a mill. He remembered the row of hives under the cherry-trees beyond the race, and how the new swarms had come out, and been sawed off with the limbs in great bunches, or called out of the air by drumming on tin pans, and how at last they had been enticed into a hive sprinkled inside with sweetened water.

So, under Philip's directions, a section of a hollow log was prepared, covered at the top and notched at the bottom, and pierced with cross-sticks to support the comb. As a temporary bench for it to rest upon, they blocked up against the back wall of the house the oak slab, which they no longer respected as a gravestone.

After it became quite dark, the bees had so far settled that a few broken pieces of honeycomb, which had been tossed off into the grass from the falling tree, were secured to sweeten the new hive, and it was finally propped up on the rubber poncho in front of the thickest bunch of bees. Tumbler was kept a close prisoner in the house, and early the next morning the bees began crowding after their queen into their new house, and by the afternoon they were carrying in the honey and wax on their legs. So it was the second night after cutting the bee-tree before the soldiers removed the hive, wrapped about with a blanket, to the bench behind the house, and got access to the honey in the broken log. There was so much of it that, after filling every dish they could spare, they were forced to empty the gold on to the earthen floor, and fill the cask with some of the finest of the combs.

What remained was given up to the bear and the bees,

who got on more pleasantly together than you can think; and in time they cleaned out the old log and scoured the wood as if they had been so many housemaids.

During the remainder of the summer the gold lay neglected in the corner together with certain wilted potatoes and fat pine-knots and the sweepings of the floor. If a shining coin turned up now and then in some unexpected place, it doubtless served to remind Coleman how handy these small tokens of exchange might be if there were any other person in all their world of whom they could buy an iron pot or an onion; or it may have suggested to the clever brain of Bromley some scheme of utilizing the pile as raw material. Worthless as the gold was in its present form, in the hands of the soldiers so fertile of resource and so clever in devices to accomplish their ends, it was not possible for so much good metal to remain altogether useless. They soon saw that, if they had the appliances of a forge, they could tip their wooden spades with gold, and make many dishes and household goods. So after the harvest they set to work in good earnest to build a smithy, and equip it in all respects as well as their ingenuity and limited resources would permit.

The first thing they did was to dig a charcoal pit, into which they piled several cords of dry chestnut wood, setting the sticks on end in a conical heap. Over this they placed a layer of turf and a thick outer covering of earth, leaving an opening at the top. Several holes for air were pierced about the base of the heap, and then some fat pine-knots which had been laid in about the upper opening, or chimney, were set on fire. These burned briskly at first, and then died down to a wreath of smoke, which was left to sweat the wood for three days, after which the holes at the base were stopped and others made half-way up the pile. Late in November the dry, warm earth about the charcoal pit was a favorite resort of Tumbler, and he tried several times to dig into the smoldering mass, with results more amusing to the soldiers and less satisfactory to himself than those of any digging he had ever tried before.

When the smoke ceased to come out of these holes at the sides, they were closed up and others pierced lower down, and so on until the process was complete.

While this slow combustion was going on, a pen was built about the fireplace of the old hut and filled in with earth to a convenient height for the forge. The flue was narrowed down to a small opening for the proper draft, and a practical pumping-bellows, made of two pointed slabs of wood and the last rubber blanket, was hung in place. Besides nailing, the edges were made air-tight with a mixture of pitch and tarry sediment from the bottom of the charcoal pit, and the first nozzle of the bellows was a stick of elder, which was very soon replaced by a neat casting of gold.

Bromley was the smith, and his first pincers were rather weak contrivances of platted wire; but after half the barrel of one of the carbines had with the head of the hatchet been hammered out on a smooth stone into a steel

MAKING A HUNDRED-DOLLAR CASTER.

plate to cover their small anvil-block, it was possible to make of the iron that remained a few serviceable tools.

While they now had good reason to be sorry that the gold was not iron, they were thankful for their providential supply of the softer metal, and Bromley toiled and smelted and hammered and welded and riveted, in the smoke of the forge and the steam of the water-vat, and turned out little golden conveniences that would have made a barbaric king or a modern millionaire green with envy. So it came about that, poor as they were, the three exiled soldiers, without friends or country they could call their own, sat on three-legged stools shod with hundred-dollar casters, and drank spring-water from massy golden cups fit for the dainty lips of a princess.

CHAPTER XIV

WHICH GIVES A NEARER VIEW OF THE NEIGHBOR CALLED "SHIFLESS"

WITH the events which closed the last chapter the three soldiers had been more than a year on the mountain. They had become thoroughly settled in their delusion, and more contented in their way of living than they would have thought it possible, in the beginning, ever to become.

The long war had come to an end in a way of its own, and without any regard for the messages flagged from Upper Bald. The soldiers of both armies had been disbanded, and the good news had found its way into the mountain settlements at about the time the bear had discovered the bee-tree.

Far and near the Union outliers had come in from their hiding-places among the rocks, and were gradually settling their differences with their Confederate neighbors, in which delicate process there was just enough shooting to prevent peace from settling too abruptly among the mountains.

In Cashiers valley there was scarcely any difference of

opinion, and the old postmaster in the Cove, who had attended strictly to his duties and never spied on his neighbors, was not molested under the new order of things, or even deprived of his office.

On the very evening when the fires were first lighted under the charcoal pit, it happened that two men were driving along a stony road which led into the valley over a spur of Little Terrapin. All day the rain had been falling steadily, and the team showed unmistakable signs of weariness, the sodden ears of the mule flapping dejectedly outward, and the steer halting to rest on every shelf of the descent, as the light wagon creaked and splashed down the mountain in full view of the wooded face of old Whiteside, now relieved boldly against a twilight sky which showed signs of clearing. The two men sat crouched on the wet seat, with a border of sodden bedquilt showing under their rubber coats, their wool hats dripping down their shining backs, and the barrels of their guns pointing to right and left out of the dry embrace in which the locks rested. As they mounted the next ridge, the major was getting a little comfort out of a spluttering pipe, and Sandy was looking hopefully between the horns of the steer at the patch of clearing sky.

"There's some humans a-outlyin' on old Whiteside to-night," said Sandy. "I 'lowed them critters had all come in."

"What yer talkin' 'bout?" growled the major.

"I 'm a-sayin'," said the other, "that there 's somebody campin' on the mountain. It 'pears to be gone now, but I certainly seen a light up thar."

The major only grunted as if the matter were of no consequence, and then both relapse into silence as the creaking wheels jolt over the rocks and grind down the mountain behind the bracing cattle. The form of the steer grows whiter in the gathering darkness. The men are evidently familiar with the country, for presently they turn off the big road into a cart-track, the sides of the wagon brushing against the dripping bushes as they push through the darkness with the fewest possible words. Now and then they see a light in the settlement, glimmering damply through the trees, and dancing and disappearing before them, as the wagon lurches and rolls upon the weary animals struggling for a foothold on the shelving rocks. At last they trot out on a sandy level and pass a log barn, where a group of men are playing cards by a fire. A little farther on a low line of lights becomes a row of windows casting a ruddy glow under the dripping trees, and shining out upon the very woodpile where, according to Philip, the man he had named "Shifless" was wont to sit and watch the milking.

"Hello, inside!" cried the major, hailing the house. "Is Elder Long to home?"

"Well, he ain't fur off," replied a tall woman in a calico sunbonnet and a homespun gown, who came out on the side porch, shading her eyes with her hand. "Jest light out o' yer hack an' come in to the fire, an' I'll carry the critters round to the stable."

Sandy and the major clambered out of the wagon upon the chip dirt, with a polite inquiry after the news, to which the woman, as she seated herself on the bedquilt and gathered up the reins, replied that "the best news she knowed of was that the war was done ended."

The travelers walked stiffly into the house, carrying their guns, besides which the major held a cow-skin knapsack by the straps, which he dropped on the floor inside the door. Both men said "Howdy" as they stalked over to the fireplace, peering from under their hats at the shadowy forms of a number of women sitting in the uncertain light, who answered "Howdy" in return; and then, while the men took off their rubber coats, one woman, bolder than the others, stirred the fire and thrust a pine-knot behind the backlog.

Presently the ruddy flames leaped up in the stone chimney and picked out the brass buttons on two butternut-and-gray uniforms, and revealed the faces of the women, evidently not over-pleased at what they saw. There was an awkward silence in the room for a moment, and then a tall man entered, followed by two others, and then a party of three. Each man carried his gun, and each said "Howdy," to which the strangers responded; but the conversation showed no signs of being general until the elder came in, unarmed, as became his peaceful calling.

His gun and powder-horn, however, were handy in a rack over the door, and as soon as his benevolent face appeared in the firelight the man Sandy advanced from the corner behind the chimney and held out his hand.

"Ye may have disremembered me, elder, in three years' time," said Sandy, rather sheepishly.

"I hain't forgot ye," said the elder, gravely, stepping back a pace and crossing his hands behind his back. "I hain't forgot ye. Been in the Confederate army, I reckon,"—at which remark there was a rustle among the elder's friends and a murmur from the women.

"Jes so," said Sandy, not at all disturbed by his cold reception; "an' likewise my friend the major—Major McKinney."

"Sir to you," said the major, with a wave of his hand.

"We're a-studyin'," said Sandy, "'bout campin' down in this yer valley—"

"We're all o' one mind here, Sandy Marsh," exclaimed Mrs. Long, who had come in from the stable. "We're Union to a man."

"That's what we be in Cashiers," snapped one of the neighbors, who was fondling his gun; and then there followed a little movement of boots and rifle-stocks on the floor, which caused the major to get upon his feet with the intention of making an explanation. There was a hostile flash in his eye, however, which Elder Long observed, and stretching out his long arm, he pointed to the major's chair.

"Now set down, comrade, do," said the elder, and then, to the others: "These two men are my guests to-night. They'll have the best that the house affords, an' ye'd better be layin' the supper-table, mother. We'll feed them an' their critters, an' welcome, an' when day comes they'll move on. Like mother put hit, we're of one way of thinkin' in Cashiers. No offense, gentlemen, but hit's plumb certain we should n't agree."

Under the advice of the elder, the men stacked their weapons together, the long rifles with the army guns; and after supper was over the whole party returned to the fire in an amiable and talkative mood, but with a perfect understanding that the two Confederates would move on in the morning.

This point having been settled, the travelers were listened to with the interest the stranger always receives in remote settlements where new faces and new ideas seldom come; and the men of the valley, who had been sullen and suspicious before they had broken bread, now laughed at the droll adventures of the major and vied with him in story-telling on their own account.

The women had mostly been silent listeners up to the time when Sandy mentioned the light he had seen on the crest of Whiteside Mountain, as they came over Little Terrapin. The major hastened to express a doubt of his companion having seen anything of the kind, which the other as stoutly contended he had seen with his eyes open, and that the light was not lightning or a stray star among the trees, but real fire.

"Ye need n't waste time studyin' 'bout that light, Sandy Marsh," said Mrs. Long, throwing the last stick on the fire, which was only a heap of glowing embers. "'T ain't worth the candle, since everybody in Cashiers knows that mountain is harnted."

"And has been ever since the little old man died up thar all by hisself," chimed in little Miss Bennett.

"I ain't a great believer in harnts," said the elder, "but

if you viewed anything like fire up thar, hit certainly wa'n't built by human hands, for there ain't no possible way for a human to git there."

"There's the bridge Josiah Woodring built," Sandy ventured to say. "I crossed over to hit myself once afore the war-time."

"Hit fell into the gorge of its own weight an' rottenness, more 'n a year back," said the elder, "an' hit 's certain that no man has set foot on the top of Whiteside since."

The fresh stick, which was only a branch, burned up and threw a flickering light on the grave faces about the shadowy room, in the midst of a general silence which was broken by the harsh voice of the mistress of the house.

"Hit's obleeged to be the harnts, an' comes 'long o' the bones o' the little old man not havin' had Christian burial up yonder."

"You see," said the elder, "his takin' off wa' n't regular, bein' altogether unbeknownst, otherwise I 'd 'a' seen he had gospel service said over him that would 'a' left him layin' easy in his grave."

"Which hit stands to reason he can't do now," put in Mrs. Long, "under that heathen inscription they do say is writ on his headstone. If he really wanted to be forgot, he 'd better left word with Jo-siah to bury him without so much as markin' the place; an' everybody knows that unmarked graves holds uneasy spirits."

"Accordin' to that doctrine, Mis' Long," said the major,

"whole regiments of harnts 'u'd be marchin' an' counter-marchin' over some battle-fields I know."

"'T ain't them that has plenty o' company that gits lonely an' uneasy," replied the woman, very promptly, "but such as lays by themselves on the tops of the mountains or anywheres in the unknown kentry."

"Old Whiteside hain't never brought luck to anybody that owned hit," said a piping voice from a niche behind the fireplace, where Granny White sat in her accustomed rocker. The old woman was the mother of the mistress of the house, and an authority far and near on all things supernatural. Her white frilled cap was just visible behind the stones of the jamb, and even the strangers listened with respect to what she had to say, in the ghostly silence and in the half-light of the dying embers.

"I 've lived in the shadder of hit for eighty year, an' ther' ain't many that 's been atop o' old Whiteside. Arter Josiah built the bridge, the Hooper horned critters lay across the gorge one summer, an' two o' the best cows lost their calves. That must 'a' been in '50. Hay, Larkin, son—'50, wa' n't hit?"

"That 's true, Aunt Lucy," said the elder; "an' a great mystery hit was at the time. Some suspicioned that the little old man might 'a' killed 'em for meat, but such of us as went up found his cabin empty, an' we could no more find him than if he had been a harnt hisself."

This statement was received in silence, which was presently broken by the garrulous voice of the old woman.

"Woe! woe! unto them that ventures onto the dangerous mountains. The last man knowed to have set foot on Whiteside was Hiram Kitchen, an' let me tell ye the harnts had a hand in burnin' Hiram Kitchen's cabin on Christmas day an' totin' him off along with his prisoners. Hit was a plain judgment ag'in' disbelief. Hay, Larkin, son? You 're l'arned in Scripture."

The elder only gazed at the feathery embers.

"Wherever the old man o' the mountain is a-layin'," continued granny, "he ain't restin' easy, an' ther' might be a reason for hit, too. He had plenty o' silver—plenty o' silver." Her voice sank to a husky whisper. "An' hit 's a monstrous lonely place up yonder—somebody might 'a' murdered him. Hay, Larkin, son? Somebody might 'a' done that."

The old woman's words had a powerful effect on the simple crowd assembled in the shadowy room. They were prone to superstitious beliefs; and if the two strangers, who had seen more of the world and had fought in real battles, were less impressed than the others, they kept a discreet silence, in which the elder rose to his feet and uttered the evening prayer, not forgetting to ask that they might be guarded from unseen enemies and from invisible dangers.

In the morning, after the two Confederates had driven away with their mule-and-ox team in search of a more congenial neighborhood, the elder seated himself on the woodpile to smoke his morning pipe and watch the milking.

"Mother," said he, after a while, when his wife came

forward between the well-filled pails, "I don't believe in harnts burnin' houses, but thar must 'a' been some spirit information pre-ju-dicial to Hiram Kitchen that I never could git through my head. The last thing I did afore I rode off to preach Granny Taylor's funeral sermon was to go up on the hill yonder an' satisfy myself that everything was quiet around Hiram's. I never let on to the postmaster that there was any Yankee prisoners around, an' if he knew of hit, he kept hit to hisself. Hit certainly looks, mother, as if the spirits had a hand in hit, an' a bad business hit was."

"That's hit, Larkin, son," said Aunt Lucy, who leaned on her staff by the fence among the great purple cabbage-heads. "When there's mischief goin' on ye can depend on hit the harnts has a hand in hit. An' hit's a fair mountain, too," she continued, shading her eyes with her hand and gazing up at the wooded mass of Whiteside, behind which the sun was rising. "Hit's fair to view, an' innocent-appearin', but there's few has set foot on the top o' hit."

The mountain, which harbored no spirits other than the guileless souls of the three deluded soldiers, was indeed fair to look upon, towering above its fellows and above the sweet valley of Cashiers. A curtain of purple haze softened the rich greens of the forest which clothed the mountain on the valley side, and now, after the rain, white clouds of vapor were beginning to puff out as if huge concealed boilers were generating steam behind the trees.

CHAPTER XV

THE GOLDEN MILL

THREE years have come and gone since the forge was built, and the three misguided patriots, still loyal to their vow and to the thirty-three stars on their dear old flag, are sitting together in the fair sunlight of a Sabbath morning on the steps of the golden mill. Tumbler the bear, very shaggy and faded as to his mangy coat, is sleeping comfortably on the dusty path that winds away to the house. Coleman's tawny and curly beard and the black hair on Bromley's face have grown long and thick, and the down which beforetime was on Philip's lip and chin now flares out from his neck and jaws like a weak red flame. Philip sits a little apart from the others, with the telescope in its leathern case strapped on his back, and there is a look of sadness in his face and in his wandering, downcast eyes.

Three years have wrought great changes in the plateau. The harvests have been abundant, and at a little distance from where the men sit purple grapes hang in great clusters from the vines which have been grown from cuttings of that solitary plant which overhung the branch on the July day when they first came down its bank with the captain of the troopers and Andy the guide.

The building of the mill has been a work of time, and it is not yet a month since Bromley emptied the first yellow grist into the flaring hopper. Two long years were spent in shaping the upper and the nether stones, and the new mill was rightly called "golden," for five thousand guineas from the mints of George the Fourth and good Queen Vic. were melted in the forge and beaten into straps and bolts and rings and bands for the wooden machinery. Gold glistens in the joints of the dripping-wheel, and gleams in the darkness at the bottom of the hopper, where the half of a priceless cavalry boot-leg distributes the corn between the grinding-stones. The hopper itself is rimmed with gold, and the circular wooden box, rough hewn, that covers the stones is bolted and belted with the metal elsewhere called precious; and from the half-roof of oak shingles to the slab floor, gold without stint enriches and solidifies the structure. It plates the handle and caps the top of the pole that shifts the water on to the wheel, and the half-door which shuts out Tumbler the bear swings on golden hinges and shuts with a golden hasp.

Healthy living and abundance of food have rounded the lusty brown limbs of the three soldiers and charged their veins with good red blood; but alas! in the midst of the abundance of nature and the opulence of the golden mill, by reason of their tattered and scant covering they are pitiful objects to look upon as they sit together in the sunlight. The smart uniforms with yellow facings are gone, and the long cavalry boots, and the jaunty caps with cross-sabers above the flat vizors; and so little remains of their former clothing that they might almost blush in the presence of the bear.

Lieutenant Coleman has some rags of blue flannel hanging about his broad shoulders, which flutter in the soft wind where they are not gathered under the waistband of a pair of new and badly made canvas trousers having the letters "U. S." half lost in the clumsy seam of the right leg and a great "A" on the back, which sufficiently indicates that they have been made from the stiff cloth of the tent called "A," and that, if required, they could easily stand alone. Such as they are, these trousers, on account of their newness and great durability, seem to be the pride of the colony. They are certainly much smarter than Philip's, which are open with rents and patched with rags of various shades of blue, and tied about his legs with strings, and finally hung from his bare, tanned shoulders, under the telescope, by a single strip of canvas.

All three of the men have hard, bare feet, and the tunic or gown of faded blue cloth which hangs from Bromley's neck shows by its age that the overcoat-capes which were sacrificed to make it were sacrificed long ago. This what-you-may-call-it is girded in at the waist by a coil of young grape-vine covered with tender green leaves, and fringed at bottom with mingled tatters of blue cloth and old yellow lining. And this completes the costume of the dignified corporal who enlisted from Harvard in his junior year,

THE GOLDEN MILL.

except some ends of trousers which hang about his knees like embroidered pantalets.

With all their poverty of apparel, the persons of the three soldiers, and their clothing as far as practicable, are sweet and clean, which shows that at least two of them have lost none of that pride which prompted them to stay on the mountain, and which still keeps up their courage in the autumn of the good year '69. And now let us see what it is that ails Philip.

Many entries in the diary for the fifth summer on the mountain, which is just over, indicate that the conduct of Philip was shrouded in an atmosphere of mystery which his companions vainly tried to penetrate. So early as March 12, 1869, we find it recorded:

"Philip spends all his unemployed time in observations with the telescope."

In the following April and May, entries touching on this subject are most frequent, and Lieutenant Coleman and George Bromley have many conversations about Welton's peculiar conduct, and record many evidences of a state of mind which causes them much annoyance and some amusement.

"May 12. Requested Philip to remove one of the bee gums to the new bench. Instead of complying with my request, he plugged the holes with grass, removed the stone and board from the top, and emptied a wooden bowl of lye into the hive, destroying both swarm and honey.

After this act of vandalism he entered the house, took down the telescope, and, slinging it over his shoulder, walked away in the direction of the point of rocks, whistling a merry tune as he went."

At another time he was asked to set the Slow-John in motion to crack a mess of hominy, and instead of spreading the corn on the rock he covered that receptacle with a layer of eggs, and hung the bucket on the long arm of the lever.

Such evidences of a profound absence of mind were constantly occurring; and if they were not indications of his desire to return to the world, his secret observations with the telescope made it plain enough that he was absorbed in events outside the borders of Sherman Territory. If questioned, he assigned all sorts of imaginary reasons for his conduct, and at the same time he held himself more and more aloof from his companions, to wander about the plateau alone.

During the previous winter, Philip had reported that one of the four young girls removed by the Confederates at the time of the capture of the officers had reappeared in the vicinity of the burned house. This fact was soon forgotten by Coleman and Bromley, who were working like beavers, pecking the stones for the mill; but to Philip it was an event of absorbing interest. Where were the others? What sufferings and what indignities had the returned wanderer endured in her long absence, and what hardships and dangers had not she braved to reach her native valley again? Gentle as Philip's nature was, he possessed in a marked degree the power to love and the hunger to be loved in return. Occasionally a man in a dungeon or on a desert island, or in the shadow of a scaffold, has devoted himself to a one-sided passion in circumstances as baffling as those that hedged in Philip.

The sight of this lonely girl wandering back to the blackened ruin in the deserted clearing furnished the dolorous lady his knightly fancy craved. A speck in the distance, he drew her to his arms in the magic lens, and consoled her with such words of sympathy and endearment as his fancy prompted. In short, he had the old disease that makes a princess out of a poor girl in cowskin shoes and a homespun frock, and had it all the worse that she kept her distance, as this one did. In the long days when storms interrupted his observations, or fog hung over the valley, he wrote tender letters to his princess on prepared leaves of his prayer-book, in which the grave responses of the Litany ran in faint lines, like a water-mark, under the burning words on the paper.

He watched Jones and the kindly neighbors (not including Shifless) clearing away the wreckage and rebuilding the Smith house between the sturdy stone chimneys. The new cabin was divided by an open covered passage, through which Philip could look with the glass to the sunlit field beyond, and watch the Princess Smith entering either of the doors opposite to each other in the sides of the passage.

This love of Philip's had sprung into being full fledged,

without any stage of infant growth like an ordinary passion. Besides its unsuspecting object, it was ample enough to take under its wings her wandering kinsfolk, dead or alive, and included the cow with the soundless bell which came to be milked in the evening by the hands of the princess herself, and then to crop the grass and lie in the dust of the road until morning.

From the time when she waved him a banner of smoke at sunrise until the firelight reddened on the cabin window, Philip came to linger almost constantly on the rocks, to the neglect of his share in the labors of the little community. When planting-time came, and hands were in demand to spade up the soil, his companions for the first time secured and hid away the telescope. For a day—for two days—Philip was uneasy, going and coming by himself, doing no work, speaking to no one, scarcely partaking of food. At last the suspense and disappointment became unendurable, and going to Lieutenant Coleman, resting from his work in the shade of a spreading chestnut, he threw himself at his feet and begged for the return of the telescope, revealing for the first time the nature of his infatuation. His lips once opened, poor Philip ran on in a rhapsody so fantastic and incoherent that the diseased state of his mind was at the same time made apparent.

In the diary for July 6, Lieutenant Coleman writes:

"An unspeakable calamity has fallen on the dwellers in Sherman Territory. Reason has been blotted out in the mind of our companion Philip, and now we are but two in the company of an amiable madman."

In view of Philip's malady Lieutenant Coleman felt it wise to humor him with the telescope, and to try the effect of more active sympathy by joining him in his observations.

After an eager examination of the clearing in the valley, "Gone! Gone!" he cried in a voice of despair. "You have driven away my princess! You hate her—you and the other one! You hate me! I'm not wise enough for your company—you and the other one. Give me back my princess—give me back—"

Taking the glass from his trembling hand, Coleman leveled it on the house in the clearing; and, happily, there stood the woman, midway of the passage, and on the point of advancing into the light.

"Take her back, dear Philip," he said, returning him the telescope. "We will never steal her again—I and the other one. See, there she is!"

With a quick movement Philip looked, and without a spoken word he fell a-laughing and crooning in his delight, in a way so unnatural and so uncanny that it was sadder to see than his excitement.

The only chance of reclaiming Philip seemed to lie in the direction of feigning sympathy with and interest in his delusion, trusting to time, in the absence of opposition, to bring him back to reason.

Never after this exhibition of petulance on the rocks with Lieutenant Coleman did he show the slightest tendency to violence. When he came in on that particular evening, the lieutenant took his hand, and in a few friendly words told him how glad he was that all was well and that the lost was found, and ordered the flag run up in honor of the occasion.

Philip looked in a dazed way at the flag, showing that that emblem had lost its old power to stir him with enthusiasm. All that summer, when his expert advice was sorely needed, poor infatuated Philip took no more interest in the construction of the golden mill than he took in the spots on the moon. He was as ignorant of the affairs of Sherman Territory as the Princess Smith, that plain, ignorant working-girl in the valley, was of his existence.

So week after week, and month after month, through the long summer and into the sad autumn days, his companions kept a melancholy watch on Philip, who wandered to and fro on the mountain, with the telescope in its leathern case strapped over his bare shoulders, as we saw him first in the shadow of the golden mill.

Scantily as the three soldiers were clad at that time, they still had their long blue overcoats to protect them from the cold of winter, and broken shoes to cover their feet; and so in the short December days poor Philip, grown nervous and haggard with want of sleep, strapped the telescope outside his coat, and wandered about the point of rocks.

The morning of January 10, as it dawned on the three forgotten soldiers,—if it may be said to have dawned at all,—cast a singular light on the mountain-top. It had come on to thaw, and the time of the winter avalanches was at hand. The sky overhead was of a colorless density which was no longer a dome; and it seemed to Philip, as he stood on the rocks, as if he could stretch out his hand and touch it. Somewhere in its depth the sun was blotted out. Ragged clouds settled below the mountain-top, and then, borne on an imperceptible wind, a sea of fog swallowed up the clouds and blotted out the valley and the ranges beyond, even as it had blotted out the sun, leaving Sherman Territory an island drifting through space.

Philip closed the telescope with a moan, and replaced it in its leathern case. Even the trees on the island, and the rocks heaped in ledges, grew gray and indistinct, and presently the thick mist resolved itself into a vertical rain falling gently on the melting snow. The strokes of an ax in the direction of the house had a muffled sound, like an automatic buoy far out at sea. Philip turned with another sigh, and took the familiar path in the direction of the ax, groping his way in the mist as a mountaineer feels the trail in the night with his feet.

The sound of the chopping ceases, and a great stillness broods on the mountain. Evidently the chopper has sought shelter from the rain. Brown leaves begin to show where the snow has disappeared on the path, so familiar to the feet of the wanderer that no sound should be needed to toll him home. But to-day, while his feet are on the mountain-top, his aching heart is in the valley. She has gone forever from the arms of the lover she never saw. He sees before him the wedding of yesterday, and in his gentleness he is incapable of hating even his successful rival. He is capable only of grief. Bitter tears fall on his breast and on his clasped hands. A great aching is in his throat, and a dimness in his suffused eyes. He throws his arms out and presses his temples with his clenched hands, and mutters with a choking sound, as he walks. He does not know that the rain is falling on his upturned face. He turns to go back. He changes his mind and advances. He is no longer in the path. He has no thought of where he goes. The blades of dead grass, and the dry seeds and fragments of leaves, cling thick upon the sodden surface of his tattered boots. He strides on absently over the ground, parting the fog and cooling his feverish face in the rain; and every step leads him nearer to the boulder face of the mountain where the great avalanches are getting ready to fall a thousand feet into the Cove below.

The events of yesterday go before him. He sees the procession come out of the church house, the women in one group and the men following in another, and he and she going hand in hand in the advance. He feels the sunshine of yesterday on his head and the misery in his heart.

Then it is night, and he sees the lights of the frolic at the cabin in the clearing. He is no longer the cheerful, happy Philip of other years, but a weakened, distracted shadow of that other Philip staggering on through the rain.

He has forgotten his soldier comrades and the meaning of his life on the mountain. He has forgotten even his patriotism and the existence of the flag with thirty-three

PHILIP ON THE EDGE OF THE PRECIPICE.

stars. Sherman Territory is receding under his feet, and the grief that he has created for himself so industriously and nursed so patiently is leading him on.

A blotch of shadows to the right assumes the ghostly form of spreading trees, the naked branches blending softly in the blanket of the fog. The gnarled chestnuts, that looked like berry-bushes while they waited at the deserted cabin on that first night for the moon to go down, give no voice of warning, and Philip comes steadily on, with the telescope strapped to his back and the load in his heart. Under his heedless feet the dead weeds and the sodden leaves give way to the slippery rock.

For a moment the slender figure crossed by the telescope is massed against the mist overhanging the Cove. Then there is a despairing cry and a futile clutching at the cruel ledge, and, in the silence that follows, the vertical rain, out of the blanket of the fog, goes on shivering its tiny lances on the slippery rocks.

CHAPTER XVI

WHICH SHOWS THAT A MISHAP IS NOT ALWAYS A MISFORTUNE

IT was still early in the day when Philip fell over the boulder face of the mountain; and when the chopping which he had heard through the fog ceased at the house, Bromley had indeed gone in, but not for shelter from the rain. He had gone to warn Lieutenant Coleman of the absence of their half-demented comrade and of the peril he ran in wandering about on the mountain in the fog. They felt so sure of finding him near the point of rocks that they went together in that direction; but before they started Philip had wandered from the path, and by the time they reached the rocks he had put the house behind him and was walking in the direction of the Cove. Finding no trace of him there, and seeing the dense mist which covered the valley and made observation impossible, they separated and went off in opposite ways, calling him by name, "Philip! Philip!" and as they got farther and farther from each other, "Philip! Philip!" came back to each faintly through the fog and the rain. They made their way to such points as he might have found shelter under, but their calls brought no response. They knew that in his peculiar state of mind he might hear their voices and make no reply, and in this was at last their only hope of his safety as they continued their search.

At twelve o'clock a wind set in from the east, redoubling the rain, but rapidly dispelling the fog. In an hour every place where he could possibly have concealed himself had been searched, and with one mind they came back to the point of rocks. They lay out on the wet ledge and looked over with fear and trembling, half expecting to see his mangled body below. They could see clearly to the foot of the precipice, and there was nothing there but the smooth, trackless snow; and then when they drew back they looked in each other's faces and knew for the first time how much they loved Philip and how much each was to the other.

They were almost certain now that he had fallen over one face of the mountain or the other. Yesterday they could have followed his track in the thin snow, but now the rain, which was still falling heavily, had obliterated one after melting what remained of the other. They went together down the ladders, and for its whole length along the base of that ledge. When they returned to the plateau, Lieutenant Coleman and Bromley were tired, and soaked with the rain, and crushed with the awful certainty that Philip had fallen over the great rock face into the Cove. They could neither eat nor sleep as long as there was a possibility of discovering any clue to his fate; and so in time they came to the slippery rock in front of the station, where the heel of his boot or the sharp edge of the telescope had made a scratch on the stone that the rain was powerless to wash out.

It was no use to call his name after that dreadful plunge, the very thought of which tied their tongues to that extent that the two men stood in silence over their discovery; and when they could learn no more they came away hand in hand, without uttering a word.

This was indeed the point where Philip had gone over the great rock; but by a strange good fortune his body had plunged into a mass of rotten snow fifty feet from the brink of the precipice. It was the snow of the avalanche making ready to fall; and through this first bank his body broke its way, falling from point to point for another fifty feet, until he lay unconscious over the roots of the great icicles which hung free from the rounded ledge below him, dripping their substance nine hundred feet into the Cove.

When he came to himself, chilled and sore after his great fall, the moon was shining softly on the snow about him and sparkling on the ice below. He had no recollection of his fall, and but the vaguest remembrance of what had gone before. It was rather as if he had dreamed that he had fallen upon the avalanche, and when he had first opened his eyes upon the snow about him and above him, he tried to reason with himself that no dream could be so real. He remembered vaguely the autumn days by the golden mill, and he knew that it was not winter at all;

and yet this was real snow in which he lay bruised and helpless. He realized that he was almost frozen, and his clothing, that had been wet, was now stiffening on his limbs. The great shock had restored his shattered mind, leaving a wide blank, it is true, to be filled in for the best part of the year that was past. He was himself again now, but where it was not at first so clear. There was nothing to be seen above beyond the snow which hung over him; but when he turned his sore body so as to look away from the mountain-side, his eyes rested on the long white roof of the Cove post-office, as he had seen it often before from the top of the plateau. Philip knew now that he was in the very heart of the avalanche. He lay on the very brink of the ice which might fall with the heat of another day's sun. At first he began to cry out for help; but his voice was such a small thing in the mass of snow against the great rock. And then he thought of the people from the hills who would come at noon of the next day to watch by the post-office to see him fall—him, Philip Welton! And then he thought of Coleman and Bromley, who must have given him up for dead; and even of his uncle at the old mill, with more of desire than he had ever felt for him before. He tried to drag himself a little from the icy brink; but his legs and arms were numb and stiffened with the cold. He began to clap his nerveless hands and stimulate the circulation of his blood by such movements as he could make. He had an instinctive feeling that the avalanche had been trembling yesterday where it clung to the great, black, vertical stain on the face of the boulder just below the trees that looked like berry-bushes from the road in the Cove. He knew that it would not fall during the night. He had no recollection of the rain. He knew that more heat of the sun was yet required to loosen it for the great plunge. It was freezing now, and every hour added solidity to the surface of the snow; and yet as he gained the power he feared to move, as the workman distrusts the strong scaffold about the tall steeple because of its great height from the ground.

Above him, ten feet away, he could see the hole in the snow through which he knew he must have fallen; and as he thought of the fearful shoot his body would have made, clearing even the great ledge of icicles, if the surface of that bank had not been rotted by some cause, his limbs were almost paralyzed with terror. The thought helped to stir the sluggish blood in his veins, and he shrank, rather than moved, a little from the awful brink where he lay. Gradually he rose to his feet and looked about him. The Cove post-office, showing its white roof through the naked trees that looked like berry-bushes in their turn, far, far below him, fascinated him until he felt a mad impulse to leap over the icicles to oblivion. Instead of yielding to this impulse, however, he covered his eyes with his hands until he found strength to turn his back on the tiny object that terrified him. If he cried out, his voice, against the rock for a sounding-board, might awaken the sleeping postmaster before his comrades on the plateau. Even in that case no help could reach him from below across the bridgeless gorge; and even if his com-

"PHILIP COULD SEE THE HOLE IN THE SNOW THROUGH WHICH HE KNEW HE MUST HAVE FALLEN."

rades were above him on the rocks, they could do nothing for him.

Should he wait there to meet certain death in the avalanche to-morrow or the next day? He thought of the cool courage of Bromley, and wondered what he would do if he were there in his place. As long as there was a foothold to be gained, he knew Bromley would climb higher, if it were only to fall the farther, and he felt a thrill of pride in the dauntless nerve of his comrade. This thought prompted him to do something for himself, and he began by whipping his arms around his body, keeping his back resolutely on the small post-office, and trying to forget its dizzy distance below him. As he grew warmer and stronger, he felt more courage. It was impossible to reach the hole in the snow through which he had come, for the broken sides separated in the wrong way from the perpendicular. He was not a fly to crawl on a ceiling.

A few yards to his right, as he stood facing the mountain, the bank through which his body had broken its way made a smooth curve to the ledge where the icicles began. As he looked at the great polished surface of the snow, the thought came to him that nothing in all the world but the soft moonlight could cling there. Hopeless as the passage by the bank was, he could reach it; and the feeling that it led away to the region above prompted him to pick his way along the narrow ledge until he could touch with his hand the smooth surface of the bank. He could only touch it with his hand, for the edge curved over his head as he stood alongside it. He felt that the bank was hard; he was unable to break its crust with his hand; and he knew that every moment it was growing harder. His strong knife was in his pocket. He drew out this and opened it with his stiff fingers. Then he began to cut his way under the bank. Beyond the first surface the snow yielded readily to his efforts; and as it fell under his feet he made his way diagonally upward until at the end of half an hour, as it seemed to him, he broke the crust of the great bank and pushed his head through into the fair moonlight. He looked up at the glaring steep above him, and it was beyond his power not to take one look back at the tiny post-office below him. If he had not been safely wedged in the bank, it would have been his last look in life. As it was, he shrank trembling into the snow, and for a whole minute he never moved a muscle.

Fortunately for his shattered nerves, it was not necessary to go out upon the surface of the bank, which was considerably less than perpendicular. He had only to cut away the crust with his knife, and so gradually work his way upward in a soft trench, leaving only his head and shoulders above the crust.

Philip felt a strange exultation in this new power to advance upward, and all his sturdy strength came to his aid in his extremity. He felt no disposition to look back at the trail he knew he was leaving in the snow. He was certain now of gaining the top of the bank, but what lay beyond he knew not. Half the distance he had fallen would still be above him. He was almost up now; but at the very top of the bank there was another curl of the snow, and once more he had to burrow under like a mole.

When Philip's head did appear again on the surface, it was not so light as before, and with his first glance around he saw that the moon was already sinking below the opposite ridge. He was almost within reach of another hole to his left; and by its appearance, and by the distance he had come, he knew it was not the same which he had seen from below, and alongside it the last rays of the moon glinted on the brass barrel of the telescope attached to its broken strap. How it had come there he had no idea, any more than he had how he had come to be lying on the ledge above the icicles where he had found himself a few hours before. It was the old familiar telescope of the station, through which the three soldiers had looked at the prisoners and at old Shifless in the valley, and it made him glad as if he had met an old friend. He stretched out his hand to draw it to him. Instead of securing it, his clumsy fingers rolled it from him on the smooth snow, and as he looked at it the telescope turned on end and disappeared through the hole in the bank. In the awful stillness on the side of the mountain, he heard it strike twice It was nothing to Philip now whether it fell in advance or waited to go down with the avalanche. And just as this thought had passed through his mind, and as he turned his eyes to the side of the cliff above him, the far-away sound of metal striking on stone broke sharply on his ear, and he knew that the telescope had been smashed to atoms on the rocks in the Cove bottom.

From where he crouched now on the snow he could see the edge of the plateau above him, and as near as he could judge it was rather less than fifty feet away. The smooth rock was cased in thin ice—so thin that he believed he could see the black storm-stain underneath. It was growing dark now, and after all his toil and hope he had only gained a little higher seat on the back of the avalanche. He saw with half a glance that it would be impossible to climb higher. He heard the wind whistle through the branches of the dwarfed old chestnut-trees over his head; and as the cold was so still about him, he knew that it was an east wind. He could go nearer to the ledge, but he could gain no foothold on the rock. In the midst of his cruel disappointment and his awful dread of the sun which would come to melt the snow next day, he felt a greater terror than he had felt when he had first found himself down below. His companions might have gone mad and thrown him over the rock. It was all a dark mystery to poor Philip. He could barely see about him now. Even the sun would be better than this darkness. It might be cold to-morrow. At any rate, it would be afternoon before the sun, however warm, could get in its deadly work on the avalanche. It never occurred to him that he was nearly famished, and he must have slept some where he sat in the snow, for he dreamed that the people were gathered at the post-office to see him fall, and a crash like the roar of battle brought him to his senses with a start. The next time he awoke, the bright sun was indeed shining, and he was stiff with the cold, as he had found himself at first. He was hungry, too, as he had never been hungry before, and the fear of starvation seemed more dreadful to him than the dread of the avalanche.

As he lay there in his weakened state, his ears were alert for the faintest sound. He thought he heard a movement on the ledge above him, and then he heard voices clear and distinct. They were the voices of Coleman and Bromley.

"Poor Philip!" he heard them say.

At first he was unable to speak in his excitement, and then he raised his voice with all the strength of his lungs, and cried, "Help! Help!"

"Is that you, Philip?"

"Yes, George! Yes! Help!"

By questioning him they learned what his situation was, and the distance he lay from the top of the ledge; for they could gain no position where they could see him. They bade him keep up his courage until they came again. It was indeed a long time before he heard their voices again speaking to him, and then down over the icy rock came a knotted rope made of strips of the canvas that remained of the "A" tent. At the end of the life-line, as it dangled nearer and nearer, were two strong loops like a breeches-buoy. Philip felt strong again when he had the line in his hand, and thrusting his legs through the loops, he called out to hoist away. As he went up, up, he clung fast with his hands to the strip of canvas; but he was too weak to keep himself away from the rock with his feet, so he bumped against it until he was drawn over the surface of the same stone he had slipped on the morning before. He saw the kind faces of his two comrades, and then he sank unconscious on the firm earth at their feet.

CHAPTER XVII

HOW THE POSTMASTER SAW A GHOST

ON the day when Philip fell into the avalanche, although it was likely to break away from the face of the mountain at any moment and come thundering down on the rocks below, not a single person came to the office to watch with the postmaster, who went outside from time to time and gazed up into the mist, and then, with a sigh of relief, returned to his arm-chair before the fireplace. In better weather he would have had plenty of gossiping company, for avalanche day was quite the liveliest day in his calendar. Despite the rain which kept pattering on the low roof, he hoped that the snow and ice would hold fast to the rock until the sun came again; but nevertheless his old ears were constantly on the alert for the crash which he feared.

On many a January day, in the years that were past, he had occupied his favorite chair in the warm sun against the east wall of the office, surrounded by his neighbors, watching the glittering mass, and noting the small fragments of ice which broke away from time to time before the final crash. He had heard nothing yet, and as the gloomy afternoon wore on he began to be almost certain that he was not to lose his holiday, after all.

The postmaster, though living so much alone, had a way of talking to himself, and on this occasion he was more talkative than ever, because of the uneasiness he felt.

"Hit 's a quare thing," he said, getting up and kicking the logs into a blaze, and then sitting down again in his sheepskin-cushioned chair. "Hit 's plumb quare."

By way of making these solitary talks more sociable, the old man had developed a clever habit of talking in dialogue, imagining himself for the time in the company of some congenial spirit, for whom he spoke as well as for himself. On this particular occasion his imaginary companion was a mountain woman for whom he had felt a sentimental regard years before, but to whom he had never told his love.

"*What 's quare, 'Manuel?* Why, look here, 'Liz'beth; I 've sorted the mail here more 'n thirty year, watchin' the avalanches fall off yonder mounting, an' in all that time I 've never set my foot onto the top of hit. *Most of us on this side hain't, 'Manuel; an' since the bridge rotted away an' tumbled into the gorge, there ain't no way o' gittin' thar.* 'Liz'beth, I 'm nat'rally a venturesome man, though I never showed it to you, 'Liz'beth, when I ought to. *That 's what ye did n't.* I 'm a venturesome man; an' this here is what I 've made up my mind to, 'Liz'beth Hough. I 'm detarmined to see the top o' that mounting afore I 'm a year older; an' I 've set the time, 'Liz'beth—nothin' personal in that, but meanin' that when the dogwood blossoms in the spring I 'm goin' to find some way to git up thar. *How 'll ye do hit, 'Manuel?* Hit 's likely I 'll fall a tree across the gorge. *Don't do hit, 'Manuel. Why not?"*

The postmaster looked wise, and put out his hand as if he were playfully touching his imaginary companion under the chin. "Why not, 'Liz'beth? *Because folks do say that the old man that lived up thar was murdered, an' that his spirit has took the form of a harnt, an' brings bad luck to such as goes up thar to disturb him."*

The postmaster rose and kicked the fire impatiently. "Bah! I 'm a bold man, 'Liz'beth, past occasions notwithstandin'. I 'm sot an' detarmined to do hit when the dogwood-trees blossom out, an' I 'm 'lowin' you 'll come an' tend the office, 'Liz'beth, while I 'm gone."

The postmaster stood with his back to the fire, looking down over his left shoulder to where the imaginary form of Elizabeth sat.

"You 'll come an' spell me, will ye, 'Liz'beth? You allus was a 'commodatin' woman. No, there ain't nothin' for ye to-day—not so much as a paper. Don't be in a hurry. This here idee of explorin' that mounting has took a powerful hold on me, sure. Nothin' that you can say will prevent me from so doin'. Well, if you must go, 'Liz'beth, I s'pose hit 's high time I was gittin' my supper. After I wash the dishes, I 'low to walk across to the big road an' see if there 's any tracks. Good-by, 'Liz'beth. *Good-by, 'Manuel."*

The postmaster was silent while he raked out a bed of

coals and set the three-legged iron skillet over the very hottest place. Then he mixed some Indian meal with milk and a pinch of salt, and having patted it down in the skillet, he put on the cover, and filled the rim with more coals and some burning embers. After he had buried a potato in the ashes, and set the coffee down to warm over, he broke out again:

"I could n't 'a' been mistaken about there bein' nothin' for 'Liz'beth. I sort o' spoke at random, knowin' that the last letter she got was in '68, month o' May." Then he stepped back so as to look through the letter-boxes, which were before the south window. "There 's nothin' in H except a linch-pin, an' I 'low that oughter be in L—no, that 's for Riley Hooper. Hello! hit 's clearin'. There 'll be a moon to-night, an' nothin' 's goin' to drap afore to-morrow."

After he had eaten, and put away the supper-things, the postmaster took down his rifle from the rack over the door, and stepped out into the clearing.

The sky was not yet free from rolling clouds, which were drifting into the east across the face of the great full moon that hung directly over the mountain. Stretching away to the seamed rock where the avalanche hung was a wide old field, broken by rocks and bristling with girdled trees, whose dead limbs wriggled upward and outward like the hundred hands of Briareus. The postmaster kept to the foot-worn trail, shuffling over the wet leaves, and glancing up now and then at the granite front of old Whiteside with great satisfaction, not only because the avalanche was safe for the night, but because he loved to think that whatever secrets the mountain held would be his when the dogwood-blossoms came in the spring.

He went as far as the big road, and finding plenty of fresh tracks, he kept on in the direction of Cashiers until he came to a cabin where the bright warm light glowed through the chinks between the logs and through the cracks about the chimney as if the place were on fire. By the merry laughter he heard and the scraping of a violin he knew that a frolic was going on, and he chuckled to think that he had in his pocket a certain letter which would be a convenient excuse for dropping in on the revelers.

The postmaster must have been welcome in his own social person over and above the favor of the letter he brought, for it was hard upon twelve o'clock when he came out and took his way homeward, feeling jollier than he had felt for many a day, and carrying a cake in a paper parcel under his arm for the coming festivities at the office.

"Who 'd 'a' thought," he said, turning to look back at the lighted cabin, where the revelry was at its height, "that I 'd 'a' been dancin' a figger this night on the puncheons with 'Liz'beth Hough? Hit sort o' took all the boldness out o' me when she come over an' asted me. I don't 'low any other human could 'a' cowed me that-a-way. I 'm a bold man under ordinary conditions prevailin' an' takin' place. I ain't easy to skeer," he continued as he resumed his walk, "leastways where men is concarned."

It was cold now, and still, and the wrinkled mud on the road was curdled with frost. The moon was well over to the west range. The last cloud had disappeared, and the stars were like jewels in the sky through the bare limbs of the trees. He was in such a rare state of exhilaration that he was more talkative than ever, and kept up a running conversation with first one neighbor and then another, until his cheerful dialogue, which had brought him to the border of his own field and in sight of the office, was rudely interrupted by the "too-hoot" of an owl somewhere among the girdled trees.

"Shet up," said the postmaster, carefully laying the cake down on the leaves, and cocking his rifle. "Good night, Riley. Linch-pin 's come; twelve cents postage stamped on the tag. *Good night, 'Manuel.* I must tend to this sassy critter, interruptin' of his betters. Where be ye, anyway? Know enough to hold yer tongue, don't ye? I 'll let ye know I 'm a bold man, leastways—" and with that he fired his gun at random. In the windless night the sharp report seemed to strike against the granite mountain and be thrown back like a ball of sound, to go bounding across the Cove, rolling into the distance.

The postmaster reloaded his gun and eased the lock down upon a fresh cap before he took up the cake, muttering at the owl, and then chuckling to think that he had silenced his rival.

He turned out of the trail to a little knoll which commanded a clear view of the granite mountain, streaked down with black storm-stains that looked like huge banners fluttering out from the shining mass of snow and ice clinging to the crest.

The postmaster gazed upward for some minutes, and then moved on in silence toward the office, under the girdled trees. The avalanche was uppermost in his mind, however, and before he had gone far he stopped on another place of vantage to take a last fond look.

"Freezin' tighter an' tighter every blessed minute," he began. "When the dogwood-trees blossom in the springtime, old rock, I'll let ye know I'm a bold—"

He never finished the sentence.

The cake and the rifle fell to the ground, and the postmaster's jaw dropped on its hinges. Cold chills ran up his back and blew like a wind through his hair, while the blood seemed to throb in his ears. He was powerless to speak. He could only gaze with his bulging eyes at the small figure which rose slowly from the roots of the great icicles and then stood motionless and black against the snow. It looked to be a figure, so small and far away in the uncertain moonlight, and yet it stood where no living man could possibly be. His first conviction was that he saw the spirit of the old man of the mountain, who, for one reason or another, was believed to rest uneasily in his grave; and when the small object began to thresh the air with its arms like the wings of a windmill, he had no further doubt that it was the dreadful "harnt" of whom 'Liz'beth had warned him. With a howl he turned and fled over the field in the direction of the office, and as he ran the owl resumed its dismal note—"Too-hoo, too-hoot." As many times as he fell down he clambered upon his feet again, and ran on, never daring to look back at the "harnt" waving its ghostly arms above the roots of the great icicles. He thought his time had come, for he had heard that men never lived who had once seen the dead; and all the time, as he ran, the mocking cry of the owl resounded through the woods.

The postmaster was staggering and breathless when he reached his door, and once inside, he shoved the wooden bolt, and leaned against the table in the center of the room. Only a few glimmering coals lighted the ashes between the iron fire-dogs. Just enough moonlight struggled through the grimy south window to show the glazed boxes, holding a paper here and an uncalled-for letter there, while the unused places were stuffed with bunches of twine, and heaps of nails, and strings of onions, and quite the dustiest litter of odds and ends filled the compartments X, Y, and Z. As the old man raised his eyes and glared around the shadowy walls, there was something which caught a fleck of moonlight high up on the chimney, but that was only the perforated cross of the churn-dasher thrust between the logs. In the north window, over opposite to the letter-boxes, his eyes fell on a wide-mouthed bottle, from whose top two dead stalks of geraniums drooped over to the shoulders of the bottle, and then spread out to right and left against the glass. With a shiver of fear, he supported himself over to his arm-chair, and sank down with his back to the object, which reminded him of the "harnt" flinging its arms against the snow on the mountain.

The postmaster had not yet found his voice. Perhaps

he feared to break the death-like stillness of the room, heavy with the sooty odor of the fireplace. For some moments he heard nothing but his own heavy breathing, and then a dull clatter, like some hard object striking on wood, came from behind the house. Instead of being startled at hearing this noise, the postmaster got upon his feet, and shuffled across the floor and out through a creaking door into a lean-to, where the moonlight poured through the loose log wall and lay in spots and stripes on the old brindle plow-steer, which was still grinding his crumpled horns against the wooden rack above his manger.

"I 've seen hit, Buck! I 've seen hit. The harnt!— the harnt!"

The postmaster's voice had come at last, and as he spoke he leaned on the shoulders of the ox, whose cold wet nose sought his groping hand.

"I hain't got long to stay. I 've seen what 't ain't good to see, an' live. I hope ye 'll git a good master when I 'm gone, Buck. Tell 'Liz'beth that I died a-blessin' of her name, with all the boldness took clean out of me. Cut off in my sins," he moaned, throwing his arms about the neck of the ox, "for seein' a harnt unbeknownst, an' hit strikin' out desperit at Jo-siah, or whoever did the murder, an' not keerin' for the avalanche no more 'n you keer for a hickory gad. Whoa, Buck, whoa," and as he spoke he patted the animal on the neck. "I 'm a-goin' to stay 'long o' you, Buck, this whole endurin' night. I 'm afeard to go back into the office."

The postmaster trembled where he stood, and a ray of moonlight, coming through a knot-hole in the slab roof, fell full on his ashen face and glaring eyes. He spoke no more for a time, except an occasional caressing word to soothe the uneasy ox, which sidled about and grated his horns against the wooden stanchions. Then, when he grew weary in that position, he climbed over into the long manger and crouched down on the cornshucks, where he could see the mild eyes of the ox, and the spots and stripes of moonlight on his tough hide. Gradually he grew calmer, and tried to put the gruesome sight he had seen out of his mind.

"I never knowed before ye was sech good company, Buck. You've got eyes like a woman, an' a heap more patience. I'll never strike ye another blow, an' if I live to see to-morrow I'll write ye a letter, an' put hit in B box, expressin' my brotherly feelin's in language more fitter than I'm able to do now."

The postmaster continued to mutter caressingly to his dumb companion, until the bars and spots of moonlight began to fade, leaving the ox in obscurity, which was the time when Philip reached the upper bank and sank down on the snow, after hearing the telescope strike on the rocks in the Cove; and both men must have fallen asleep at about the same time.

It was mid-forenoon when the postmaster awoke, and a man was standing over him, shaking his shoulder. The man was coming home from the frolic at the cabin, and finding the front door bolted, had come around to the shed. He had the cake and the gun, which he had found in the field.

"What in the name o' sense are ye doin' here at this time o' day, 'Manuel? Come outen that manger."

The postmaster obeyed in a dazed sort of way, and when he was on his feet he shook the straws and bits of corn-husks from his clothing, the old brindle ox looking at the two men with his mild eyes from his place in the corner.

"What made ye drap these things out in the field, 'Manuel?" said the man.

"Come into the office, Jonas," said the postmaster, leading the way; and then he told the other of the fearful sight he had seen.

The sun was warm after the rain, and soon others began to come,—men and women,—and he told his story again and again, to the awe and amazement of his simple listeners.

"I seen a quare streak down the long bank, as I came through the woods," said one man; "I did sure." And then they all went out into the field where the gun and the cake had been found. Sure enough, there was a dull line plainly to be seen on the smooth crust of the snow. They all agreed that this was the track of the "harnt," who had amused himself in the night-time by climbing up and sliding down on the face of the avalanche.

The story spread through the settlements, and no man was bold enough thereafter to think of bridging the gorge to get upon the haunted mountain.

CHAPTER XVIII

KNOWLEDGE FROM ABOVE

WHEN Philip awoke, after having swooned at the feet of his comrades when his rescue was accomplished, he lay in the delicious warmth of his bunk. The late afternoon sun streamed in at the window over his head, and Coleman sat watching at his side. Bromley was stirring the fire, which was burning briskly on the hearth, and the smell of gruel was in the room. The station flags and the crossed sabers brightened the space above the chimneypiece. The map hung on the opposite wall, and over it the old flag with thirty-five stars seemed to have been draped just where it would first catch his waking eye.

Strangely enough, the immediate cause that awoke Philip was a dull boom which made the faces of his comrades turn pale, and which was no less than the fall of the avalanche on which he had passed the night and the best part of the day before.

Philip, if he heard the sound at all, was not sufficiently awake at the time to understand its awful meaning; and without noticing the pallor of his comrades, he weakly put out his hand, which Coleman took in his own with a warm pressure, and Bromley came over to the side of the bunk and looked doubtingly into his face. Neither of his comrades uttered a word.

"Give me the gruel," said Philip; "I was never so hungry before. And don't look at me so, George; I'm not mad."

After he had eaten, he talked so rationally that Coleman and Bromley shook each other's hands and laughed immoderately at every slightest excuse for merriment, but said not a word of the delusion which had so lately darkened Philip's mind. They were so very jolly that Philip laughed weakly himself by infection, and then he asked them to tell him how he had fallen over the mountain without knowing it.

In reply to this question, Coleman told him that he had been sick, and that he must have walked off the great rock in the thick fog.

Philip was silent for a space, as if trying to digest this strange information, and then with some animation he said:

"Look here, Fred! The funniest part of this whole dark business was when I had climbed up to the top of the great bank. There, alongside a hole in the snow, lay our telescope. When I put out my hand to take it, it rolled away through the opening in the snow; and the Lord forgive me, fellows, I heard it ring on the rocks at the bottom of the Cove."

With this long speech, and without waiting for a reply, Philip fell off into a gentle doze.

Coleman and Bromley, having no doubt now that Philip's mind was restored, because he seemed to have no recollection of the princess or of his strange behavior on the mountain for the year that was past, were very happy at this change in his condition. As to the telescope, they regarded its fall as a very dangerous matter, and a catastrophe which might bring them some unwelcome visitors. But, then, it was possible that it had fallen among inaccessible rocks, and would never be found at all. If any one should come to disturb them, they might hear of some unpleasant facts of which they would rather remain in ignorance. Now that nearly five years had passed since the great war, they thought that whoever came would not exult over them in an unbearable way, or rub insults into their wounds. They knew that some of the mountaineers had been Union men; and although they would never seek communication with them, a connection formed against their will might result to their advantage. They had a good supply of the double eagles left. Somebody held title to the mountain, they knew; and if the telescope did bring them visitors, they could buy the plateau from the deep gorge up, and pay in gold for it handsomely, too. Then they could send down their measures to a tailor and have new uniforms made to the buttons they had saved— that is, if the tailor was not a secessionist too hot-headed to soil his hands with the uniform of the old, mutilated, and disgraced Union. Then, too, they could buy seeds and books and a great many comforts to make their lives more enjoyable on the mountain.

And so it came about that, when month after month passed and nobody came, the three soldiers were rather disappointed. They resolved to save what remained of their minted and milled coins against any unforeseen chance they might have to put them in circulation; and now that they thought of it, it would have been much wiser to have melted the coins of the United States and saved the English guineas. If, however, the world had not changed greatly since they left it, they believed the natives in the valley below would accept good red gold if the face of the old boy himself was stamped on the coin.

When Philip was quite himself again, by reason of his knowledge of milling he took entire control of the golden mill. In the cold weather his old overcoat was dusty with meal, as a miller's should be; and in the summer days plenty of the yellow dust clung to the hairs on his arms and in his thin red beard.

It is a Sunday morning in September again, and, to be exact with the date,—for it was a very important one in their history,—it is the fifth day of the month in the year '70. The three soldiers are standing together by the door of the mill, dressed very much as we last saw them there, and engaged in an animated conversation.

"An egg," said Lieutenant Coleman, facing his two comrades, and crossing his hands unconsciously over the great "A" on the back of his canvas trousers, "as an article of food may be considered as the connecting-link between the animal and the vegetable. If we had to kill the hen to get the egg, I should consider it a sin to eat it. What we have to do, and that right briskly, is to eat the eggs to prevent the hens from increasing until they are numerous enough to devour every green thing on the mountain."

"I am not so sure of that," said Philip, toying with his one dusty suspender; "we could feed the eggs to the bear."

"We could, but we won't," said Bromley, shaking some crumbs from the front of his gown. "When nature prompts a hen to cackle, do you think we are expected to look the other way? Why, Philip, you will be going back on honey next because bees make it. We are vegetarians because we no longer think it right to destroy animal life. We not only think it wrong to destroy, but we believe it to be our duty to preserve it wherever we find it. Don't we spread corn on the snow in the winter for the coons and squirrels? Come, now! We are not vegetarians at all. We are simply unwilling to take life, which leaves us to choose between vegetable diet and starvation. Now, then," said Bromley, spreading out his bare arms and shrugging his shoulders, "of the two, I choose a vegetable diet; but if I could eat half a broiled chicken without injury to the bird, I'd do it. That's the sort of vegetarian I am."

"Nonsense!" said Philip. "You're a dabster at splitting hairs, you are. It was uphill work making a vegetarian of you, George; but we have got you there at last, and you can't squirm out of it."

"Give it to him, Phil!" cried Coleman. "Hit him on the salt!"

"Exactly!" continued Philip, taking a swallow of water from a golden cup, and addressing himself to Bromley. "When the salt was gone you thought you'd never enjoy another meal, did n't you?—and how is it now? You are honest enough to admit that you never knew what a keen razor-edge taste was before. I'll bet you a quart of double eagles, George, that you get more flavor out of a dish of common—"

At that moment a bag of sand came through the branches of the tree which shaded the three soldiers as they talked. There was a dark shadow moving over the sunlit ground, and a rushing sound in the air above. Their own conversation, and the noise of the water pouring from the trough over the idle wheel and splashing on the stones, must have prevented their hearing human voices close at hand. Rushing out from under the trees, they saw a huge balloon sweeping over their heads. The enormous bag of silk, swaying and pulsating in the meshes of the netting, was a hundred feet above the plateau; but the willow basket, in which two men and one woman were seated, was not more than half that distance from the ground. The surprise, the whistling of the monster through the air, the snapping and rending of the drag-rope with its iron hook, which was tearing up the turf, and which in an instant more scattered the shingles on the roof of their house like chaff, and carried off some of their bedding which was airing there—all these things

"RUSHING OUT FROM UNDER THE TREES, THEY SAW A HUGE BALLOON SWEEPING OVER THEIR HEADS."

were so startling, and came upon them so suddenly, that they had but short opportunity to observe the human beings who came so near them.

Brief as the time was, the faces of the three strangers were indelibly impressed upon their memory, and no portion of their dress seen above the rim of the basket escaped their observation. The woman, who appeared to be perfectly calm and self-possessed, kissed her hand with a smile so enchanting, lighting a face which seemed to the soldiers to be a face of such angelic beauty, that they half doubted if she could really belong to the race of earthly women they had once known so intimately. The men were not in like manner attractive to their eyes, but seemed to be of that oily-haired, waxy-mustached, beringed, and professorish variety which suggested to them chiropodists or small theatrical managers.

Notwithstanding the rushing and creaking of the cordage, the voices of the men in the balloon had that peculiar quality of distinctness that sound has on a lowery morning before a storm. Indeed, each voice above them had a vibration of its own which enabled the soldiers to hear all commingled and yet to hear each separately and distinctly. The hurried orders for the management of the balloon were given in subdued tones, and uttered with less excitement than might have been expected in the circumstances, yet the words came to the earth with startling distinctness.

When they saw the soldiers, the taller of the men, who wore the larger diamond in his shirt-front, put his hand to his mouth and cried in deafening tones:

"'Skylark,' from Charleston, 3:30 yesterday."

At the same time the beautiful lady, laying her hand on her breast as if to indicate herself, uttered the words:

"New York! New York!"

Even while they spoke, their voices grew softer as the balloon sped on, the great gas-bag inclined forward by the action of the drag-rope, and its shadow flying beneath it over the surface of the plateau. As soon as the two professors saw the danger which threatened the log house, they began to throw out sand-bags from the car, and the lady clung with both hands to the guy-ropes. It was too late, however, to prevent the contact, and the lurch given to the basket by the momentary hold which the grappling-hook took in the roof of the house threw several objects to the ground, and on its release the balloon rose higher in the air, having a "U. S." blanket streaming back from the end of the drag-rope. The property they were bearing away was seen by the men in the car, and the rope was taken in with all speed; but a fresh breeze having set in from the east, the balloon was swept rapidly along, so that it was well beyond the plateau when the blanket fluttered loose from the hook.

The soldiers ran after it with outstretched arms until they came to the edge of the great boulder, where they saw their good woolen blanket again, still drifting downward with funny antics through the air, until it fell noiselessly at the very door of the Cove postmaster.

The balloon itself was by this time soaring above the mountains beyond the Cove, and they kept their eyes on the receding ball until it was only a speck among the clouds and then vanished altogether into the pale blue of the horizon.

The soldiers had not seen the objects tumble out of the car when the drag-rope caught in the shingles of their house, and the thoughts of their wrecked roof and lost blanket had the power for the moment to displace even the image of the beautiful lady, whom they could never, never forget. The passage of the balloon had at first dazed and awed, and then charmed and bewildered them, leaving them in a state of trembling excitement impossible for the reader to conceive of.

They no longer had the telescope with which to observe the surprise of the Cove postmaster when he found the gray blanket with "U. S." in the center; but they had the presence of mind to get behind trees, where they waited until he came out. He looked very small in the distance when he came at last, but they could see that the object was a man. It was evident, from his not having been out before, that he had not seen the balloon pass over. He seemed to stoop down and raise the blanket, and then to drop it and stand erect, and by a tiny flash of light which each of the soldiers saw and knew must be the reflection of the sun on his spectacles, they were sure he was looking at the top of the mountain and thinking of the east wind. There was no help for it; and when he disappeared into the office with their blanket, they chinked the gold in their pockets; for they carried coin with them now, and thought that an opportunity might soon come for them to spend it. As they moved away in the direction of the house, they were sorry that the drag-rope of the balloon had not fastened its hook in the plateau; for they believed they were rich enough to buy the coats off the backs of the two men, and the diamonds in their shirt-fronts if they had cared for them.

As the three soldiers neared the house, they began picking up the sand-bags, stenciled "Skylark, 1870." Philip, who was in the advance, had secured three, which he suddenly threw down into the grass with a cry of joy; for at their feet lay a book with an embellished green cover. The three were almost as much excited as they had been when they discovered the contents of the keg which they had dug out of the grave of the old man of the mountain, and instantly had their heads together, believing that they were about to learn something of the condition of the old United States, and even fearing they might read that they no longer existed at all. They were so nervous that they fumbled at the covers and hindered one another; and between them, in their haste, they dropped it on the ground. When they had secured it again and got their six eyes on the title-page, imagine their surprise and disgust when they read, "A Treatise on Deep-Sea Fishing"!

"Bother deep-sea fishing!" exclaimed Philip.

"Hum!" said Coleman, "it will work up into paper for the diary."

Bromley said nothing, but looked more disgusted than either of his comrades, and gave the book, which they had dropped again, a kick with his foot.

Their disappointment was somewhat relieved presently, for in the chips by the door of the house they found a small hand-bag of alligator leather marked with three silver letters, "E. Q. R." The key was attached to the lock by a ribbon; and as soon as the bag could be opened, Coleman seized upon another small book which was called "The Luck of Roaring Camp." The author was one Francis Bret Harte, of whom they had never heard before. The book was a new one, for it bore "1870" on the title-page, and the leaves were uncut except at a particular story entitled "Miggles."

Besides this book the bag contained numerous little trinkets, among which the most useful article was a pair of scissors. They found three dainty linen handkerchiefs with monograms, a cut-glass vinaigrette containing salts of ammonia, a rag of chamois-skin dusty with a white powder, a tooth-brush, and a box of the tooth-powder aforesaid, a brush and comb, a box of bonbons, a pair of tan-colored gloves, a button-hook, and an opened letter addressed to Elizabeth Q. Rose, No. 165 West 130th street, New York city.

The letter bore the postmark, "Liverpool, August 12," and was stamped at the New York office, "August 20, 8 P. M." Here was evidence of progress. *Eight days from Liverpool to New York!*

The envelop had been torn off at the lower right-hand corner in opening, so that it was impossible to tell whether the letters "U. S." or "C. S." had been written below "New York." The soldiers cut the leaves of the book, and glanced hurriedly over the pages without finding anything to clear up the mystery which interested them most. They sat down on the woodpile, sorely disappointed, to talk over the events of the morning; and presently they began clipping off their long beards with the scissors, and using the brush and comb, to which their heads had so long been strangers. The experience was all so strange that but for the treasures left behind, not counting the "Treatise on Deep-Sea Fishing," they might have doubted the reality of the passage of their aërial visitor.

When it came to a division of the trifles of a lady's toilet, the well-known prejudice of the world below concerning a second-hand tooth-brush was cast to the winds by Bromley, while Lieutenant Coleman, who had some qualms of conscience, was better satisfied with the rag of chamois-skin for the same purpose. The vinaigrette and the gloves fell to Philip. They had just a handkerchief apiece, and nobody cared for the button-hook.

The letter found in the bag was a subject of heated discussion, and from motives of chivalrous delicacy remained for a long time unread. George Bromley contended that its contents might throw some light on the subject which the books had left in obscurity, while Lieutenant Coleman shrank from offering such an indignity to the memory of the angelic lady of the air. It was finally agreed that Bromley might examine and then destroy it, Lieutenant Coleman declining to be made acquainted with its contents.

They never quite understood the association of the

beautiful lady with the two men, of whom they had but a poor opinion. When Bromley suggested that to their starved eyes a cook might seem a princess, his comrades were sufficiently indignant, and reminded him of her literary taste, as shown by the quality of the new book found in the bag.

After all, they had learned nothing of the great secret that vexed their lives. Was there still in existence a starry flag bearing any semblance to this one which was now floating over the mountain? Was it still loved in the land and respected on the sea?

To men who had seen it bent forward under the eagles of the old republic, gray in the stifling powder-clouds, falling and rising in the storm of battle, a pale ghost of a flag, fluttering colorless on the plain or climbing the stubborn mountain, human lives falling like leaves for its upholding—this was the burning question.

CHAPTER XIX

THE CAVE OF THE BATS

WHEN the nine small gunny-sacks stenciled "Skylark, 1870," were emptied on the floor of the house, the crustacea of the Atlantic's sands had found a resting-place on the summit of Whiteside Mountain, and might yet furnish evidence to some grave scientist of the future to prove beyond a doubt that the sea at no very remote period had surged above the peaks of the Blue Ridge. Starfish, shells, and bones, and fragments of the legs of spider-crabs, horseshoe-crabs, and crayfish, and some very active sand-fleas afforded much scientific amusement to our exiles, and brought vividly to mind the boom of the sea and the whitebait and whales that wiggle-waggle in its depth.

Neither the telescope nor the army blanket with "U. S." in the center, nor the two combined, had brought any visitors to the three soldiers, nor any information of the real state of affairs in the United States, which would quickly have terminated their exile.

The very pathetic and amusing volume of stories found

in the alligator-skin bag caused more tears and healthy laughter than the soldiers had given way to since their great disappointment, and actually brought about such neglect of the October work on the plantation that more than half the potato crop rotted in the ground.

On the 21st of that month in this very balloon year, the area of Sherman Territory was extended by the addition of half an acre of rocks and brambles on the boulder side of the mountain, and afterward of much more, as will be shown in due time.

The twenty-first day of October in the year '70, then, was a lowery day. A strong, humid wind was blowing steadily across the mountain and soughing in the boughs of the pines, while the low clouds, westward bound, flew in ragged rifts overhead. It was a pleasant wind to feel, and the rising and falling cadence of its song reminded the soldiers of a wind from the sea. In the successive seasons they had gleaned the grove so thoroughly, even cutting the dry limbs from the trees, that they were now obliged to search under the carpet of needles for the fat pine-knots which formerly lay in abundance on the surface.

At the extreme southern end of the tongue of land on which the pines grew, a solitary stump clung in the base of the cliff. The outer fiber of the wood had crumbled away, leaving the resinous heart and the tough roots firmly bedded in the soil. They had been chopping and digging for an hour before they loosened and removed the central mass. Continuing their quest for one of the great roots which ran into the earth under the cliff, George dealt a vigorous stroke on the rotten stone and earth behind, which yielded so unexpectedly that he lost his footing, and at the same time his hold on the ax, which promptly disappeared into the bowels of the earth. They heard it ring upon the rocks below with strange echoes, as if it had fallen into a subterraneous cavern. At the same time the wind rushed through the opening in a current warmer than the surrounding atmosphere, and brought with it a strong, offensive smell, as if they had entered a menagerie in August. As soon as the soldiers recovered from their surprise they set vigorously to work for the recovery of the ax, attacking the loose earth with their gold-tipped shovel and with the tough oaken handspike with which they had been prying at the stump. Their efforts rapidly enlarged the opening, and presently the great root itself tumbled in after the ax. Philip ran to the house for a light, and by the time he returned with a blazing torch, Coleman and Bromley had enlarged the opening under the cliff until it was wide enough to admit their bodies easily. All was darkness, even blackness, within, and the rank animal smell was as offensive as ever, so that Philip held his nose in disgust.

By passing the torch into the opening of the cavern they could see the ax lying on the earthen floor ten feet below, and to the right the overlapping strata of granite seemed to offer a rude stairway for their descent. George entered at once, with the torch in one hand, and in the other the handspike with which to test his footing in advance. In another moment he stood on the hard floor by the ax. and the light of his torch revealed the rocky sides of the cavern stretching away to the south along the side of the mountain. Coleman provided himself with one of the fattest of the pine-knots, and descended into the cavern after Bromley. With some hesitation Philip followed.

The resinous smoke of the torches relieved the subterraneous atmosphere somewhat of its offensive animal odor, and the flames flooded the walls and ceiling with light. Their voices, calling to each other as they advanced, sounded abnormally loud, and seemed to fill the space about them with a cavernous ring in which they detected no side echoes which would indicate lateral chambers branching off from the main passage. By the current of air flaring the torches back toward the opening they had made, they knew that the passage itself must be open to the day at its other end. The roof seemed to be about eight feet above their heads, although at times it drew nearer, and occasionally it retired to a greater altitude, but never beyond the searching illumination of their torches.

Presently, as they advanced, their attention was drawn to brown masses of something like fungi clinging to the rock overhead, but partaking so closely of the color and texture of the stone that they seemed, after all, to be but flinty lumps on the roof. As Bromley, who was in front, came to a point where the ceiling hung so low as to be within reach, he swept the flame of his torch across one of these brown patches, and straightway the stifling air was filled with a squeaking, unearthly chorus, and with the beating of innumerable wings. Scorched by the flame and blinded by the light, many of these disabled creatures, which proved to be a colony of bats, fluttered to the floor, and dashed against the bare feet of the soldiers with a clammy touch that made the cold chills rise in their hair.

This was too much for Philip, who turned back to join Tumbler in the open air at the mouth of the cavern. At the same time, however, the offensive odor was accounted for, and Bromley and Coleman had no further fear of meeting larger animals as they advanced. As a lover of animals, George was shocked at the cruel consequences of his rash action; as a bold explorer, however, he pushed on into the gruesome darkness at a pace that soon left Coleman's prudent feet far behind. The latter had a wholesome fear of treading on some yielding crust which might precipitate him to other and more terrible depths.

The way seemed to turn somewhat as they advanced; for at times the light of George's torch vanished behind the projection of one or the other wall, and at such times Coleman called eagerly to him to wait. Bromley's cheery voice, evidently advancing, came ringing back so distinctly that his companion was reassured by his seeming nearness. Once, when the darkness had continued for a long time in front, Coleman began to be alarmed at the thought that Bromley's torch must have gone out, and then the fear that he might have fallen into some fissure in the rocks made him cold about the heart.

Lieutenant Coleman was now picking his way more

"BEYOND THE ILLUMINATION OF HIS TORCH HE SAW TWO GLEAMING EYES."

gingerly than ever, and holding his light high above his head, when, to add to his terror, he thought he heard something approaching behind him. Sure enough, when he turned about, in the darkness of the cavern just beyond the illumination of his torch he saw two gleaming eyes. The eyes were fixed upon him, and the head of the animal moved from side to side, but came no nearer. He would have given worlds for the carbine. His blood ran cold in his veins at the thought of his terrible situation. He was utterly helpless, hemmed in by the rocks. It was impossible to go back. He could only go forward. He remembered then that the fiercest of wild animals, even lions and tigers, kept back in the darkness and glared all night with their hungry eyes at the fires of hunters. He was safe, then, to go on, but a dreadful conflict was in store for the two men if the animal should follow them out of the cavern.

Bromley's torch now reappeared in the distance. Coleman was too terrified to call, but instead moved on in silence, occasionally flaring his torch behind him, and always seeing the gleaming eyes when he looked back. Try as he would, he could get no farther from them. There were occasional stumbling-blocks in the way, and once or twice he encountered rocks which he was obliged to pass around. Whenever Coleman turned and waved the torch, the animal whined as if he too were in fear.

Terrified as Lieutenant Coleman was, he could not help noticing that the brown colonies of bats now appeared more frequently on the stone ceiling, and presently the air grew perceptibly fresher as he advanced. He began to realize the presence of a gray light apart from that of his torch; and finally coming sharply around a projecting rock, he saw the welcome light of day streaming in through a wide opening in the rocks, and at one side, thrust into a crevice, George's torch was flaring and smoking in the wind. Coleman placed his torch with the other, hoping that the lights would continue to protect them from the animal, and then he sprang out of the cavern into the sweet open air, with that joyous feeling of relief which can be understood only by one who has passed through a similar experience.

George was standing in the dry grass, with a great stone in each hand, as if he already knew their danger and was prepared; but when Coleman told him in hurried words what they had to expect, he dropped the stones, and they began to look about for a place of safety. It was not far to a high rock upon which they both scrambled, and then Bromley let himself down again, and passed up a number of angular stones for ammunition. Whatever the mysterious beast might be, they could keep him off from the rock for a time, but they were not prepared for a siege. They had little to say to each other, and that in whispers, as they strained their eyes to look into the entrance to the cavern. Bromley, however, was softly humming a tune, and just as Coleman looked up at him in astonishment he dropped the stones from his hands and burst into laughter; and sure enough, there in the mouth of the cavern stood their tame bear, Tumbler, wagging his head from side to side just as Coleman had seen the mysterious eyes move in the darkness, and, moreover, he was still licking his chops after the feast he had made on the bats.

Lieutenant Coleman had been so alarmed at first, and then so gratified at the happy outcome of his adventure, that he had not noticed the character of the stones which Bromley had been handling. It was not until his attention was called to a flake of mica that he looked about him on the ground, to see everywhere blocks and flakes of what is commonly called isinglass. They could have something better than wooden shutters for their windows now.

By a certain gnarled chestnut which overhung the cliff above them, growing out of the hill near the spring, they estimated the length of the subterraneous passage to be not less than a quarter of a mile. The sun, which had broken through the clouds, indicated by the angle of his rays that the afternoon was well past. They now thought it advisable to retrace their steps through the unsavory cavern. In view of the stifling passage, Coleman inhaled deep drafts of the sweet outer air, and shuddered involuntarily at the necessity of repeating the experience, even when he knew the animal now following him was only stupid old Tumbler. George handed him a piece of the mica to carry, and his careless, happy mood indicated that he returned to the subterraneous passage as gaily as if it were a pleasant walk overland. As they drew near the entrance to the cavern, with the bear shambling at their heels, an indefinable dread of trouble ahead took possession of Coleman. It might have been the absence of the resinous smell of the torches. At all events, they were presently standing in the gruesome half-light before the empty crevice, through which they could see their pine-knots still burning fifty feet below in an inner cavern. As their torches had burned to the edge of the rock they had fallen through the opening. They were without fire, and if they should succeed in striking it with their flints, they had no means of carrying it a hundred yards into the darkness.

The situation was frightful. Outside, the perpendicular cliff rose a matter of sixty feet to the overhanging trees of the plateau, and close to the south ledge, which towered above it. The two men and the bear were prisoners on this barren shelf of rocks, with a quarter of a mile of subterraneous darkness separating them from food and shelter—from life itself. Was it their destiny, Coleman thought, to die of starvation among these inhospitable rocks, hung like a speck between the plateau and the valley, watched by the circling eagles and by the patient buzzards, who would perch on the nearer tree-tops to await their dissolution? The very thought of the situation unmanned him.

Lieutenant Coleman was not a man to shrink from enemies whom he could see; but the darkness and the dangers of the half-explored cavern terrified him. Corporal Bromley, on the other hand, was only made angry by the loss of the torches; and the livid expression of his face reminded his comrade of the morning when they had received the news of General Sherman's death before the works at Atlanta. In a moment, however, he was calm.

EXPLORING THE CAVE OF THE BATS.

Without a word, he walked away among the rocks, and when he came back he held in his hands a lithe pole ten or twelve feet long.

"Not a very interesting outlook, Fred, for a man who would rather be eating his supper," said George, trying the strength of his pole; "but you must be patient and amuse yourself as best you can."

Lieutenant Coleman stared at Bromley in speechless amazement as he disappeared into the cavern, carrying the pole across his breast. It was something less than courage—it was the utter absence of the instinct of fear which the others had so often noticed in his character. Would he succeed the better for the very want of this quality with which the All-wise has armed animal life for its protection? Perhaps.

The bear was snuffing about Coleman as if he were trying to understand why he remained; and when he failed to attract his attention, he turned about and shambled after Bromley.

Although Coleman was deeply concerned by the dangers which threatened his comrade, he reasoned with certainty that wherever Bromley was, he was as calm as an oyster, regarding his progress as only a question of time and some bruises.

To keep his mind away from the cavern, he rose mechanically, and began to gather up the fragments of mica and heap them together. For an hour he threaded his way among the rocks, thus employed. The glittering heap grew larger, for the supply was quite inexhaustible, and he discovered fresh deposits on every hand.

It was now grown quite dark, and he made his way to

the mouth of the cavern, vainly hoping to see a star advancing in the darkness, but only to meet a flight of bats wheeling out into the night. Carefully he crept back and seated himself on a smooth stone by the side of his store of mica, and imagined himself a hunter in the middle of a trackless desert, dying for a drop of water beside a princely fortune in accumulated elephants' tusks. When he looked up the dark mass of the tree-crowned cliff cut softly against a lighter gloom; but when he turned his eyes away from the mountain, the sky or the clouds, or whatever it might be, seemed to surround him and press upon him. Oh, for one star in the distance to lift the sky from his head; or, better yet, the calm face of the moon, and the touch of its yellow light on tree and stone! Instead of anything so cheerful, a patter of raindrops met his upturned face, as if in mockery of his wish; and then the rain increased to a steady downpour, beating from the east, and he knew the autumnal equinox was upon them. He reflected that George might never feel the rain. Miserable thought! What if he were to perish in the darkness, separated from him and from Philip, after having lived so long together! Coleman might have sought shelter in the mouth of the cavern; but he was indifferent to the rain falling on his bare back and canvas trousers.

How long he had been waiting, two hours or three, he had no means of telling. His watch had long since ceased to run. Up on the plateau they had noon-marks at the house and at the mill, and at night, when it was clear, they went out and looked at the seven stars. He was thoroughly drenched by the rain, which had now been falling for a long time. Certainly George should have returned before this, if all had gone well with him. And then his mind returned to the contemplation of that other possibility with a perverseness over which he could exercise no control. He saw Bromley lost in some undiscovered byway of the subterraneous passage, groping his way hopelessly into the center of the mountain; knowing that he was lost when, go which way he would, his pole no longer reached the walls. He saw him retracing his steps, now going this way, now that, but always going he knew not whither, too brave to yield to despair.

Then he saw him in a lower cavern, where he had fallen through the floor, groping about the rough walls with bleeding hands and staring eyes, patiently searching for a foothold, his indomitable pluck never failing him. Horrible as these fancies were, others more dreadful oppressed his half-wakeful mind; for he was so tired that in spite of the rain he lapsed into a state of unconsciousness, in which he dreamed that the roof of that suffocating cavern, covered with the brown blotches of bats, was settling slowly upon George, until he could no longer walk erect. Lower, lower it came in its fearful descent, until it bumped his head as he crawled. Now the roof grazes his back as he writhes on his belly like a snake.

"Fred! Old boy! Fred!"

And there stood Bromley in the flesh, as calm as if nothing unusual had happened, the raindrops hissing in the flame of his torch.

CHAPTER XX

THE STAINED-GLASS WINDOWS AND THE PRISMATIC FOWLS

OWING to the difficulties of the passage through the cave of the bats, and the utter barrenness of the rocky half-acre which lay at its other end, the three soldiers never entered it again during the fall and winter which followed its discovery. The two blocks of isinglass which they had brought away on their first visit were ample for their purpose; and as soon as they had secured their supply of fat pine-knots for light in the long winter evenings, they set about constructing two windows to take the place of the sliding boards which closed those openings in the cold, snowy days. It is true, they could not look out through the new windows, but much light could enter where all had been darkness before. Time was nothing to the soldiers in these late autumn days; and, indeed, the more of it they could spend on any work they undertook, the more such work contributed to their contentment and happiness. They wished to have their windows ornamental as well as useful; and it was Philip's suggestion that they should try an imitation of stained glass.

They had some of the carbine cartridges left; and as they no longer killed any creatures, the bullets would supply them with lead to unite the small pieces of isinglass and outline their designs. One of the mica blocks chanced to be of a pale-green color, and they made many experiments to produce reds and blues. Oxid of iron, or the common red iron-rust, gave a rich carmine powder, which, mixed with the white of an egg, adhered to the inner side of the small panes. They found a few dried huckleberries, from which they extracted a strong blue by boiling. They could procure yellow only by beating a small bit of gold to the thinnest leaf, which they pasted upon the flake of mica. The reds and blues as they applied them were only water-colors; but the inner side of the glass was not exposed to the rain. After the one square window, which looked toward the Cove and consequently let in the afternoon sun, was finished in a fantastic arrangement of the three rich colors, bordered by pale green, it was decided, with great enthusiasm, to reproduce in the opposite window their dear old flag with its thirty-five stars. To do this, they cut away the logs on one side until they had doubled the area of the opening. They managed to stiffen the frame on the inner side with strips of dogwood, which made a single cross against the light, leaving the blue field of stars unobstructed.

It was a great comfort to their patriotic hearts to see the sun glowing on their United States window when they awoke in the morning, or to see the ruddy firelight dancing on the old flag, if one of them came in from the mill or the branch in the evening. In fact, when this work was finished, the three soldiers, wrapped in their faded blue overcoats, were never tired of walking about outside their house, in the chilly November evenings, to admire their first art-work illuminated by the torch-light within. Their tough, bare feet, insensible to the sharp stones and the gray hoar-frost, wore away the withered grass opposite to each of their stained-glass windows; but the patch of trodden earth outside the window which showed the glowing stripes and gleaming stars of the old flag was much the larger.

Otherwise their prospects for the winter were by no means as brilliant as their windows; for besides the failure in the potato crop, the white grubs had made sad havoc with their corn in two successive plantings, and the yield in October had been alarmingly light. Even the chestnuts had been subject to a blight; and altogether it was what the farmers would call "a bad year." The fowls had increased to an alarming extent, considering the necessity of feeding so many, and as winter approached their eggs were fewer than ever. The case was not so bad that it would be necessary to shorten their rations, as they had done before the harvest of the first year; but with so many mouths to feed, there was danger that they would find themselves without seed for the next planting. Then, too, there was a very grave danger that before spring these stubborn vegetarians would be forced to resort to broiled chicken, spiced with gunpowder, which was nearly as repulsive to their minds as leaving the mountain and going down into a triumphant Confederacy.

The bear, at least, would require no feeding, and with the very first snow old Tumbler disappeared as usual, making the soldiers rather wish that, for this particular winter, hibernation could be practised by human animals as well as by bears.

After Christmas the weather became unusually cold, and the winds swept with terrific force across the top of the mountain. The snow was so deep that the path they dug to the mill was banked above their heads as they walked in it, and the mill itself showed only its half-roof of shingles and its long water-trough above the surface of the snow. From the trough huge icicles were pendent, and it was ornamented with great curves of snow; and when Philip set the wheels in motion, a gray dust rose above the bank, and the whir of the grinding as heard at the house was subdued and muffled like the very ghost of a sound. The soldiers dug open spaces to give light, outside the stained-glass windows, and through these the evening firelight repeated the gorgeous colors on the snow.

From the path to the mill they dug a branch to the forge, and tunneled a passage to the water, from which they broke the ice every day. Short as was their supply of corn, they were obliged to feed it to the fowls with a lavish hand as long as the deep snow remained. This necessity kept them busy shelling the ears by the fire in the warm house, after they had brought them in from the mill or the forge, and half a gunny-sack of corn was thrown out on the snow at the morning and evening feeding.

Since the hut of the old man of the mountain had been made into a forge, the fowls had roosted in the branches of the old chestnuts, and had got on very well, even in the winters that were past. With full crops, they seemed to be thriving equally well during the severe cold which attended the period of deep snow.

The 15th of January in the new year, which was 1871, was the first of a four days' thaw. The sun beamed with unusual heat on the mountain, and under his rays the snow rapidly disappeared, and the ground came to light again with its store of dry seeds. The three-pronged tracks of the fowls were printed everywhere in the soft top-soil, where they scampered about in pursuit of grubs and worms. On the fourth day the avalanche fell from the great boulder into the Cove, with the usual midwinter crashes and reverberations, which reminded Philip of his narrow escape the winter before.

On the evening of this fourth day the thaw was followed by a light rain, which froze as it fell, and developed into a regular ice-storm during the night. When the three soldiers looked out on the morning of the 19th, they found their house coated with ice, and the mountain-top a scene of glittering enchantment. Every tree and bush was coated with a transparent armor of glass. The lithe limbs of the birches and young chestnuts were bent downward in graceful curves by the weight of the ice, which, under the rays of the rising sun, glittered and scintillated with all the colors of the rainbow. Every rock and stone had its separate casing, and every weed and blade of grass was stiffened with a tiny shining overcoat. The stalks on the plantation stood up like a glittering field of pikes.

Despite the difficulty of walking over the uneven ground and the slippery rocks, they made their way, not without occasional falls, to the western side of the plateau to observe the effect in the Cove. Philip was in raptures over the prismatic variety of colors, picking out and naming the tints with a childish glee and with a subtle appreciation of color that far outran the limited vision of his comrades, and made them think that Sherman Territory had possibly defrauded the world below of a first-rate painter.

As they turned back toward the house, after their first outburst of enthusiasm over the beauties of the ice-storm, Bromley remarked that it was strange they had not been awakened as usual by the crowing of the cocks. Indeed, the stillness of the hour was remarkable. It was strange that while they had lain in their bunks after daybreak they had not heard the cocks answering one another from one end of the plateau to the other.

Usually they heard first the clear, ringing note of some knowing old bird burst loud and shrill from under the very window, and then the pert reply of some upstart youngster who had not yet learned to manage his crow drifting faintly back from the rocks to the west; then straightway all the crowers, of all ages and of every condition of shrillness and hoarseness, tried for five mortal minutes to crow one another down; and when one weak, far-away chicken seemed to have got the last word, another would break the stillness, and the strident contest would begin again.

Perhaps they had heard all this and not noticed it. They were so used to the noise; it was like the ticking of a clock or the measured pounding of the Slow-John; but it was certain that nothing of the kind was going on at present.

In leaving the house they had been so enchanted by the hues of the ice-storm that they now remembered they had not so much as turned their eyes in the direction of the roost. When they came upon the brow of the hill which overlooked the mill,—which was a silver mill now,—the limbs of the trees which stretched along the bank beyond were crowded with the fowls, at least four hundred of them, sitting still on their perches. Philip, who fell down in his eagerness, and rolled over on the ice, remarked as he got upon his feet that it was too knowing a flock of birds to leave the sure hold it had on the limbs to come down onto the slippery ground.

As the soldiers came nearer, however, they noticed that their fowls in the sunlight were quite the most brilliantly prismatic objects they had seen; for their red combs and party-colored feathers made a rich showing through the transparent coating of ice which enveloped them like shells and held them fast to the limbs where they sat. Whether they had been frozen stiff or smothered by the icy envelop, they were unable to determine; but they could see that all the fowls had met with a very beautiful death, except two or three of the toughest old roosters, who had managed to crack the icy winding-sheet about their bills. One of these, who had more life in him than the others, made a dismal attempt to crow.

Bromley hastened to get the ladder from the mill, and the hatchet, and wherever a living bird was to be seen he put up the ladder regardless of the dead ones, which broke off and fell down, and chipping the ice about its claws, removed it tenderly to the ground. In the end the three soldiers carried just two apiece, one under each arm, of these tough old veterans into the house, and not daring to bring them near the fire, set them up to thaw gradually against the inner side of the door. Then they made a pot of hasty-pudding for their own breakfast; but before they touched it themselves they fed a little of it, steaming hot, to each reviving old bird. In fact, the poor fowls looked so much like colored-glass images, when tilted against the door, that, fearing at any moment they might topple over and break into fragments, they laid each rooster carefully on his side, where the ice melted by degrees into sloppy pools on the floor.

The oldest of these unhappy survivors had come up the mountain tied to a pack-saddle, and consequently was more than six years old. He was big of frame and tawny of color, and had long, sharp spurs curved like small powder-horns, and his crow when he was in good health proclaimed him the leader of the flock. The other five cocks, although but a trifle younger, belonged to the next generation, for they came of the first summer's hatching. Their plumage was red and black, and their long, sweeping tail-feathers cased in ice would certainly have been snapped off if they had had the least power to move their bodies. As the ice melted from their heads, they looked about the house with their round red eyes, and otherwise lay quite helpless on their sides, their claws drawn up to their crops, and curved as they had been taken from the limbs.

The soldiers looked on, full of sympathy, and fed their patients now and then with a small portion of warm pudding; and finally, remembering their medicine-chest, which they had never yet had occasion to use, they waited patiently until the ice melted, so that they could handle the fowls without danger of breaking, and then they held each rooster up by the neck and dosed him with a spoonful of whisky and quinine.

Following this prescription they laid the old birds in a row on a warm blanket, sufficiently elevating their heads, and covering them up to their bills, and left them to sleep and sweat after the most approved hospital practice.

And now, having done their duty by the living, they went outside to look at the dead, which were, if possible, more beautiful than ever. The sun was unusually warm, and by this time everything was dripping and glittering in the light, which was half blinding, and the thin ice was snapping everywhere as the lightened limbs sought to regain their natural positions. As to the dead fowls, a few had fallen to the ground, but most of them remained rigidly perched on the great limbs, dripping a shower of raindrops upon the ice below. Here and there, where a few rays of the sun had found passage to a particular limb, a section of the icy coating had turned so that a half-dozen fowls hung heads downward, or the casing of a hen had melted, while her claws were still frozen fast, leaving her to lop over against her neighbor for support.

By afternoon they began to fall off the branches like ripened fruit, and drop on the ground with a thud like apples in an orchard on a windy day. It was a dismal sound in the ears of the three soldiers, and a sad sight to see the heaps of dead fowls as they accumulated on the ground.

The military training of these young men had taught them to make the most of every reverse, and if possible to turn defeat into victory; and so they fell to work and plucked off a great quantity of soft feathers, and all the next day was spent in skinning the breasts, which they would find some way to cure and make into covers for their beds, or even garments for themselves. A portion of the carcases they tried out over the fire, and made a brave supply of oil for the mill, and then the poor remains were thrown over the cliff.

The six old roosters remained alive in a crippled and deformed condition, some having three stumpy toes to a foot, and others two or one, on which they wabbled and limped about with molting feathers and abbreviated combs, the most dismal-looking fowls that can be imagined. The old yellow patriarch was paralyzed as to his legs and thighs, so that he was nearly as helpless as a tailor's goose, and had to be set about and fed like an infant. For the five red ones Bromley fixed a roost in the corner of the house behind the door, where some of them had to be helped up at night, and where they crowed hoarsely in the morning, over against the window of the stained-glass flag.

Philip, in pursuance of a brilliant idea which he kept to himself, selected a dozen of the new-laid eggs which they happened to have in the house, and put them away in a warm place where no breath of frost could reach them. When the first warm days of spring came, he made a nest of corn-husks and feathers on a sunny shoulder of rock. Into this nest he put the eggs he had saved, and covered them with the old paralyzed yellow rooster, who had never been known to move from where he was set down since the night he was frozen on the limb. The indignant old bird certainly gave Philip a look of remonstrance as he left him in this degrading position; and when Philip came a few hours later to feed him, this cunning old rooster, strengthened perhaps by his outraged feelings, had in some way managed to turn over so that he lay on his side on the rock, his helpless claws extending stiffly over the nest. As often as he was set back he managed to accomplish the same feat, when if left on the ground he would sit for a week where he was placed, as stolid and immovable as a decoy-duck.

The loss of the fowls had left an abundance of corn for planting; but when the warm days came after this trying winter, it was a queer sight to see the three soldiers walking about the top of the mountain, with their five sad roosters wabbling at their heels.

CHAPTER XXI

A SCRAP OF PAPER

THE long, cold winter of 1870, which froze all the fowls except the six sad roosters, and followed the failure of the potato and corn crops, was also disastrous to the bees. The hives had increased to a fine long row in the years that followed the capture of the first swarm discovered by Tumbler, the bear, and the honey had been a welcome addition to the soldiers' simple fare; but the cold weather had destroyed every swarm, leaving only bee-bread and some half-consumed old combs from which the dead bees had fallen in a dry mass upon the bench below.

While Coleman and Bromley were engaged in planting, Philip was making an effort to find a new bee-tree. He had noticed some bees buzzing about the wild flowers on the ridge by the old flagging-station, and he determined to "line" them by a method he had seen his uncle practise when he was a boy in Ohio. He made a little box with a sliding cover, into which he put a small honey-comb, and taking the old yellow rooster under one arm for company,—or perhaps for luck,—he went over to where the flowers grew near the northern end of the plateau. He set down the old rooster on the ground, and opened the box on a stone in front of him, and waited, watching his bait. It was something like fishing in the old mill-pond, of which he had once been fond, and he found a singular fascination about watching the opening in the box as he used to watch his bobber. The June weather on the mountain was like May in the Ohio valley, and the sweet smell of the flowers carried his mind back to his old home. He had no longer to wait for the first nibble than he had waited in the old days for the first stir of his cork and the spreading ring on the water. A bee lighted on the lid and then made his way down into the box. After loading his legs with honey, the bee reappeared, and rising into the air, flew away to the south. Philip followed the small insect with his eyes, and then, picking up the old rooster, he came on for a hundred yards in the same direction, and set his bait as before. This time he had two bees in his box, and when they had loaded themselves they flew away in the same direction as the first. They disappeared so soon above the tree-tops that he thought the swarm was not far away; but every time he advanced, the loaded bees continued to fly south, until he had moved the paralyzed old rooster by easy stages the whole length of the plateau; and the bees, which came in greater numbers now, rose into the air and flew in a "bee-line" over the top of the southern cliff.

Philip was disgusted at this result of his bee-hunt, as

any fisherman, after wading to his middle in a cold river to humor a fine trout, might be, to lose his victim at last in the foaming rapids; but he knew to a certainty that there was a bee-tree somewhere beyond the thus far unscalable southern cliff.

For the present the vision of honey was abandoned, and the economy of the camp, where food was now alarmingly low, was cunningly exercised to discover edible things in lieu of the corn, which, after the planting, was all stored in the nine gunny-sacks which had fallen from the balloon. The sacks were piled one upon another in a small heap behind the hopper in the mill, and the six sad roosters had to shift for themselves as best they could, except the old fellow who was paralyzed, and for him they gathered grubs and worms, and saved the crumbs that fell from the table.

It appeared possible to the minds of the soldiers that the liver-colored slabs of fungus which grew out of the sides of the chestnut-trees and the birches might be as palatable and nourishing as mushrooms. They broke off one of these pieces one day, which was shaped like the half of an inverted saucer, and was moist and clammy on the under side. They had a suspicion that such things were poison. They had never heard of any one eating the like, and after they had stewed it in their camp-kettle, inviting as its odor was, they sniffed and hesitated and feared to taste it. In the end they shook their heads, and spilled the contents of the kettle on the ground, where as soon as their backs were turned Tumbler and the five sad roosters fell to devouring the rejected food.

When the soldiers discovered what their domestic animals were about, the bear was licking his chops and the old roosters were waltzing about in the grass picking up the last morsels of the feast. They regretted their carelessness, and rather expected that before night the old paralyzed rooster would be their only living companion on the mountain.

When, however, the bear and the five sad roosters survived the test, and seemed rather to flourish on the new food, the soldiers took heart, and found the fungus not only good, but so much like meat that it was quite startling to their vegetarian palates.

After eating all of this peculiar food-product that grew on the plateau, they gleaned the field above the deep gorge, and as a last resort they made a hunting expedition to the half-acre of rocks and brambles where they had found the mica. Terrible as the passage through the cavern had at first seemed to the mind of Lieutenant Coleman, the lapse of time and a better acquaintance with the interior of the subterraneous tunnel made it but a commonplace covered way to the field of mica. Not that the soldiers had any further use for the mineral wealth which was so lavishly strewn among the rocks. It was as valueless to them now as the button-hook found in the hand-bag of alligator-skin. To go now and then through the underground passage, however, if only for the purpose of looking at the world outside from the view-point of their newest territorial possession, was a temptation which no landed proprietors could resist. The little shelf afforded them a glimpse to

"HE WAS DOWN ON HIS HANDS AND KNEES UPON THE TURF."

the south of the Cove road, which on account of certain intervening trees was not to be had from the plateau above. Several cabins could be seen smoking in the small clearings which surrounded them, but since the telescope had gone into the avalanche with Philip there was but poor satisfaction in looking at them.

They found a single piece of the liver-colored fungus growing on the root of a half-decayed old chestnut, and even this they regarded as well worth their journey. They spent some time wandering about the mica shelf, and when Lieutenant Coleman and Philip were boring their torches into the ground, one after the other, to rid them of the dead coal, and getting ready for the start back, Bromley, who had been poking about among the rocks, called to them in a tone of voice that indicated a pretty important discovery in the stone line. He was down on his hands and knees on the turf, boring his toes into the soil, and as his comrades approached him, he exclaimed:

"I have n't touched it yet. Just come here and look!"

Naturally, Coleman and Philip thought he had found some curious reptile. Instead, however, of this being the case, Bromley was kneeling over a scrap of newspaper which was impaled on a dead twig under the shelter of a rock where neither the sun nor the rain could reach it. The torn fragment was scarcely larger than the palm of one's hand, and snugly as it was now protected from the weather, it was yellow from former exposure, and the print was much faded, so that parts of it were illegible. It was possible, however, to decipher enough of the small advertisements on the exposed side to show that it was a Charleston paper, and they knew of course that it must have come by the balloon almost a year before. Undoubtedly it had lain for a long time on the plateau above, exposed to the storms, before the wind had tossed it over the cliff and landed it in such a wonderful way on the twig under the cover of the rock.

On the reverse side most of the print was fairly legible. The scrap was torn from the top of the paper, and had on it a capital G, which was the only letter left of the name of the paper. The line below read: "September [date of month gone], 18–0." The center column was headed:

"FOREIGN WORLD

"*The Hon. Charles Snowden, M. P., goes down with his yacht — Earthquake in Spain; four distinct shocks felt — No dam e done — Movement of specie*

"London, September 4. The steam-yacht of the Honorable Charles Snowden, M. P., which was wrecked yesterday off the old Head of Kinsale on the south coast of Ireland, was this morning looted by thieves. The ri , plate, carpets, upholstery, and fittings, as well as quantity of storage, sails, and stores, were taken. Lights were seen from the mainland at two o'clock this morning, when a heavy sea was running.

"Later. The Hon. Charles Snowden and the first officer of the boat lost their lives by the swamping of the raft on which they had embarked.

"Madrid, September 4. Four distinct shocks of an earthquake this morning were felt in the province of Granada, in the south of Spain. Coming as t shocks have, twenty-four hours later than the ances reported on the coast of Italy by y
 ws, would indicate that the disturbance
    No damage is reported. In
        from the vineyards."

What remained of the right-hand column bore, to the soldiers, these surprising words, in sentences and parts of sentences:

"*Local Happenings — Charleston —*
R. E. Lee as General — Sherman at the War Office

"The controversy just concluded between the Couri Mercury on the strategic merits of the two command developed nothing new. The Sherman cam
ending at the city of Atlanta
ably discussed and with
justice to the dead comma
The great·March to the Sea, b
More brilliant achievement
of the war and its
in another colum
South is satisfie
happy endin"

When Coleman and Philip caught the first glimpse of the scrap of paper, tattered and yellow, they believed it to be some fragment of the Blue Book which they themselves had discarded. The exposed surface was almost as free of print as if it had been treated with potash, and looked as insignificant as a dried leaf or a section of corn-husk. Bromley, on the other hand, had examined it more closely, and just as Coleman began to laugh at him, he put out his hand and removed the scrap of paper from the twig which held it fast; and as he turned it over to the light, he was nearly as much surprised as his companions.

The three were down on their knees in an instant, eagerly devouring the words of the head-lines; and Philip being on the right, it happened that his eyes were the first to fall on the name of General Sherman.

"'Sherman at the War Office'!" he cried. "What does that mean?"

"It means we have been deceived," said Coleman. "I—"

"Hurrah!" cried Philip, leaping up and dancing about until the rags of his tattered clothing fluttered in the sunlight. "Hurrah! Uncle Billy is alive! He never was killed at all! If that message was false, they were all false—all lies! lies! What fools we have been! We must leave the mountain to-morrow—to-night."

"We have been the victims of an infamous deception," exclaimed Lieutenant Coleman. "Let us go back to the house at once, and determine what is to be done."

Against this undue haste Bromley remonstrated feebly, for he himself was laboring under unusual excitement. His eyes were so dimmed by a suffusion of something very like tears—tears of anger—that he could read no further for the moment, and he put the paper carefully into his pocket, and picked up his torch and followed his comrades sulkily into the cavern.

Upon Bromley's peculiar character this new revelation had a depressing effect. He still entertained doubts. If the new hope was finally realized, his joy would be as deep and sincere as that of the others. For the present, the thought that they might have been deceived all along angered him. He had an inclination to stop even then and examine the paper more fully by torch-light; but the underground passage was long, and the pine-knot he carried was burning low. He felt obliged to hasten on after Coleman and Philip, who were now considerably in advance. They were still in view, however, and as he held the torch to one side that which he saw far up the narrowing cavern had a softening effect on his conflicting emotions. He even laughed at the grotesque exhibition; for the small figures of Coleman and Philip were dancing and hugging each other and dashing their torches against the rocks in a way that made them look like mad salamanders in the circling flames and sparks.

Such reckless enthusiasm was a condition of mind which George could not understand; but the possibility occurred to him that in their wild excitement they might set fire to the house as a beacon-light to the people in the valley; for they could never get away from the plateau without help from beyond the deep gorge.

To prevent, if possible, any rash action on the part of

his more excited comrades, Bromley hurried his pace, and, in the effort to overtake them, soon found himself leaping over obstacles and dodging corners of the rocky wall in a wild race, which tended to excite even his phlegmatic nature. As he ran on, that magical sentence, "Sherman at the War Office," stood out in black letters before his eyes. What war office? If the paper referred to the war office of the United States, it certainly would have so designated a department of a foreign government. If there were two governments, it would be necessary to say which war office was meant. If the old government in whose military service he had enlisted as a boy had regained its own, the phrase "Sherman at the War Office" would be natural and correct; and with this triumphant conviction he ran on the faster. On the other hand, if the Confederacy had gained everything!—at the sickening thought his feet became so heavy that his speed relapsed into a labored walk, and the oppressive air of the cavern seemed to stifle him.

He would reach his companions as soon as possible, and compel them to examine the scrap of paper and weigh its every word. It was beginning to dawn upon Bromley that they had acted like children; and when he finally came out at the entrance to the cave of the bats into the subdued light under the dark pines, he found Philip and Coleman waiting for him, and clamoring for another look at the scrap of paper.

There was not much to read in the fraction of a column that interested them most, but Philip and Coleman were determined to twist the reading to the support of their new hopes, and Bromley naturally took the opposite view, heartily wishing, however, that the others might prove him mistaken. There was something in the reading of the broken sentences that tended to quiet the enthusiasm of Lieutenant Coleman, and when Bromley could make himself heard, he called attention to the second sentence, "The Sherman campaign ending at the —— Atlanta, ably discussed," and "Justice to the *dead commander.*" What dead commander, if not General Sherman? If he had lived his campaign would not have ended at Atlanta. It was evident that there had been a newspaper controversy in Charleston on the merits of two campaigns by Sherman and Lee—the Atlanta campaign and the March to the Sea—whatever that might be. The latter, Bromley thought, was clearly some achievement of Lee's. And then he remembered his prophecy on the night when they had changed the name of the plateau from Lincoln to Sherman Territory.

"It proves," cried Bromley, "just what I foresaw: that, after the capture of Washington, Lee led his army across Maryland, Pennsylvania, and New Jersey, living on the country, to meet the foreign allies of the Confederacy in the harbor of New York. It was certainly a brilliant military movement. Look," he cried, when the others were silent, "'South is satisfied—happy ending—'"

"But," said Philip, still obstinate, "what do you make of those five words, 'Sherman at the War Office'? How do you get around that?"

"Why, my dear boy," said Bromley, "this is only the heading of a newspaper article. It does not mean that General Sherman was at the war office in person. It simply refers to General Sherman's record in the War Department."

After all their excitement, Coleman and Philip were obliged to give way to the convincing evidence revealed in the broken sentences. They were too tired by this time to consider the bits of foreign news, or notice the dates, and it was quite dark when they reached the house and went dejected and supperless to bed.

The next morning they got down the map, and looked ruefully at the States which Lee must have devastated in his triumphant march. With the consent of the others, Bromley took a pen and traced the probable route by Baltimore, Philadelphia, and Trenton to the Jersey coast of New York harbor. Bromley was determined to lay out the line of march by Harrisburg, and was restrained only by physical force, which resulted in blotting the map at the point where his clumsy line was arrested. They agreed, however, that Lee's victorious army had undoubtedly camped on the lower bay and along the Raritan River, in the country between Perth Amboy and the old battle-field of Monmouth. They were convinced that the map was utterly wrong, for after such a march it was doubtful if there were any United States at all. The disaster appeared more overwhelming than ever, and they hung the map back on the wall—in another place, however, for it was discovered that the rain had beaten through

G

FOREIGN WORLD

LOCAL HAPPENINGS, CHARLE B. E. LEE AS GENERAL — S MAN AT THE WAR OF

THE HON. ... NOWDEN, M. P. — GOES DO
WITH HIS YACHT — EARTHQUAKE IN SPAIN
DISTINCT SHOCKS FELT — NO DAM
... SPECIE.

London, September ... The yacht of the Honorable ... CHARLES SNOWDEN, M. P., which was wrecked yesterday off the head of Kinsale, on the south coast of Ireland, was this morning boarded by thieves. The rich plated carpets, upholstery and fittings, as well as a large quantity of canvas, sails and stores, were taken. Lights were seen from the mainland at two o'clock this morning, when a heavy sea was running.

LATER — The Hon. CHARLES SNOWDEN and the first officer of the boat lost their lives by the swamping of the raft on which they had embarked.

MADRID, September 8th. — Four distinct shocks of an earthquake this morning were felt in the province of Granada, in the south of Spain. Coming as ...
shocks have, twenty-four hours later than the ...
... reported on the coast of Italy, by ...
would indicate that the disturbance ...
... damage is reported. ...
from the vineyards.

The controversy just concluded between the Mercury on the strategic merits of the two developed nothing new. The Sherman ending at the City of Atlanta ably discussed and with justice to the dead com... The great March to the sea, More brilliant achievements of the war and its in another colum South is satisfi happy ending

"THE SCRAP OF PAPER."

the logs and run down across the Pacific side. Poor as it was, they were determined to preserve it.

It was not until late in the afternoon of the day on which they had altered the map that the three soldiers returned to the examination of the scrap of paper which they had agreed from the first could have reached the mountain-top only by falling from the balloon the year before.

"How is this?" cried Coleman, pointing excitedly to the dates of the foreign telegrams. "This piece of newspaper could not have come by the balloon. The balloon passed over the mountain on September 5, having left the city of Charleston, as declared by the tall aëronaut, at 3 : 30 o'clock of the afternoon before, which was the 4th of September. Look at the dates for yourself," he continued, handing the paper to Bromley. "Was n't the Honorable M. P. drowned on the morning of September 4? Can't you read there that the earthquake in Spain was on the 4th?"

"What of that?" said Bromley; "you can't make out the date of the paper."

"I don't care what the date of publication was," replied Coleman. "If it came by the balloon it was published before September 5. Now please tell me how it could bring European news of the 4th."

"Hum!" said Bromley, somewhat puzzled. "If it had been published on the 3d, it could n't bring news of the 4th — that's certain."

"I have it," cried Philip; "Fred has got the dates of the diary more than a week out of the way. We thought the balloon passed on September 5. It was nearer the 15th."

"No," exclaimed Coleman, glaring at Philip; "there is no mistake in the record; not a date is omitted. Leap-year was added to the days in February when it came around. *I* make a mistake in the date! No, sir! There is no mistake. Whatever happens, I will stand on the rec—"

"You are right, old man," cried Bromley, interrupting him; "and the paper proves it. Don't you see the point? They have got the Atlantic cable down at last, and working like a charm. The paper was published on the 4th of September. It was an afternoon paper, and this piece fell from the balloon on the 5th of September."

They agreed that this was wonderful as explaining without doubt what at first seemed impossible, and at the same time verifying the accuracy of the dates in the diary which Lieutenant Coleman had conducted for more than six years at the time the balloon passed. Coleman and Bromley remembered distinctly the unsuccessful attempts at laying the Atlantic cable in the summer of 1858, and the fame of Cyrus Field as its projector; and now by the discovery of this scrap of yellow and tattered paper they were made aware that the great project had been continued to a successful issue. Possibly they were the more keenly interested in this evidence of progress in the world below from having been themselves connected with telegraphing in a modest way. At all events, they regarded the yellow messenger as one of their most significant possessions, and skewered it against the chimney through the very hole made by the dry twig which had held it so long under the cover of the rock awaiting their inspection.

It was near the end of July now, and the spears of corn which had thrust their tiny dark-green lances out of the mellow earth had first turned yellow, and then withered and died. A few plants here and there had escaped the ravages of the grubs, but the yield would be insignificant, and they were good enough farmers by this time to know that to plant more would be only a waste of the small store of food they had left. If the lives of the fowls had been spared, it might have been different. At the time the ground had been spaded the five sad roosters had done all that lay in their power to exterminate the grubs, but their capacity was not the capacity of the four hundred fowls of the season before.

The potatoes had suffered, though in less degree, from the same hidden enemy; and unless something could be done to increase their food-supply the three soldiers would be reduced to the verge of starvation before another winter came around. They might yet be forced to abandon their vegetarian principles and to eat the bear and the six old roosters. Rather than do anything so inhuman, they declared they would find some way to open communication with the people in the valley. They might easily have planted a larger area in former years, and stored up corn against a failure in the crop, but of this they had never thought.

The morning after they had discovered the scrap of

paper on the mica shelf, they all went solemnly to the mill and watched Philip set the machinery in motion and grind the first of the nine small sacks of corn. The whir of the wheels and the hum of the stones in the midst of the splashing of the water outside made the sweetest of music in their ears, but the song of the mill was of brief duration. When the last kernels began to dance on the old cavalry boot-leg in the bottom of the hopper, the miller shut off the water, and in the silence that followed the three soldiers looked ruefully at the small heap of yellow meal on the floor of the dusty bin. It was not more than enough to keep themselves and the paralyzed old rooster alive for a week. If they relied upon the meal alone, in nine weeks they would be out of bread, and the golden mill would be a useless possession.

Discovery was their only hope of further subsistence. They had made some remarkable finds in the past, but at the beginning of their eighth year on the mountain it would seem that no secrets of the plateau had escaped the prying eyes of these enterprising young men. Philip reminded his comrades of the bee-tree, which was undoubtedly stored with honey, beyond the southern cliff, but this they had always regarded as impassable. From the mica shelf they could see that it was a narrow ledge, and not a higher level; and although the small shelf extended a trifle beyond it, the soldiers had seen no way of scaling the rocks which rose from the brambles and mica, so as to reach the territory beyond the southern ledge.

They had never seen these rocks from above, nor any

part of the brambly half-acre, for the reason that the edge of the plateau shelved off in a dangerous incline of smooth granite, which it was not possible to look over. Otherwise they might have discovered the outside half-acre long before they found the cavernous path which led to it. Bromley now proposed to be lowered to the outer edge of the shelving rock by means of the breeches-buoy which had lifted Philip from his perilous seat on the avalanche. It was not at all a dangerous experiment, and as soon as he was in a position to examine the rocks below the base of the southern cliff, he saw a narrow ledge which would afford a sure foothold, and which led away upward until it was lost behind the rocks. Although invisible from below, it could be reached by their longest ladder.

Whether the path along the ledge would enable them to reach the top of the mountain to the south remained to be determined. They were all on fire with the fever of exploration; and they had no doubt that the rich bee-tree would reward their efforts with new stores of honey. That night, by means of the canvas strap, they lowered their ladder over the ledge until it rested on the mica shelf.

Next morning, bright and early, Philip got out his small honey-box, and would have taken the old paralytic rooster along but for the implements it was necessary to carry. Besides their torches, in passing through the cavern their hands would be full with the ax and a pail for water, and another in which to bring back the honey.

It was a clear July day, with a soft south wind breathing on the mountain; and when the three soldiers arrived on their brambly half-acre they found their ladder leaning safely against the rocks where they had lowered it. After they had smothered their torches and laid them by to await their return, they tried the ladder, which proved to be too short by a couple of rungs to reach the path on the cliff. At first they thought they should be obliged to return and make a longer one, but Lieutenant Coleman was something of an engineer on fortifications, and under his directions they fell to work building a platform of stones and timber, which afforded the ladder a secure foundation and raised it safely to the brow of the ledge.

Bromley went ahead with the ax, and Coleman and Philip followed with the pails. The soldiers had brought along their overcoats for the fight with the bees; and when they put them on after the rough exercise of handling the stones, they found them rather oppressive to their brown shoulders, whose summer costume usually consisted of one suspender. Bromley was very red in the face as he pushed along on the rocky path, cutting away a root or an overhanging limb which obstructed their passage.

CHAPTER XXII

THE DESERTED HOUSE

THE path up which the three soldiers were climbing was not a path at all in the sense of its having been worn by the feet of men or animals. It was at first a narrow ledge, and then the dry bed of a watercourse, which overflowed for a few days when the snows melted in the spring, and was walled in by an outer ledge, and turned upward at an easy incline which offered no serious obstacle to the progress of the explorers. The soldiers halted midway, and took off their oppressive overcoats and wiped their red faces.

The top of the mountain beyond the southern wall was about half the area of their own plateau, and, to the consternation of the three soldiers, in the very center of the tract stood a log house flanked by some tumble-down sheds. This unexpected discovery was so startling that they retreated below the bank for consultation. They had no doubt that the bees Philip had lined came from the hives of these people. If there were a bee-tree at all, they would not be allowed to cut it. Lieutenant Coleman was at first disposed to return without revealing themselves to the strangers. Their curiosity, however, was so roused, and their desire was so great to learn something of their neighbors, that the three soldiers crept back until only their heads were above the edge of the bank, and their wondering eyes fixed on the house. There might be women there, and from a sense of modesty each man got back into his old blue overcoat. They talked in husky whispers as they stared through the bushes, expecting every moment to see some one come out for a pail of water or an armful of wood.

"There's a man down there by the shed," whispered Philip; and so timid of their kind had the soldiers become after seven years of seclusion, during which they had not spoken to a human being, that they ducked their three heads in a tremble of excitement. Presently Bromley looked again, and almost laughed out loud; for the man was only a stump with something thrown over it that stirred with the wind.

There was no smoke from the chimney; but it was midway between breakfast and dinner, and fire was not to be expected at that hour in midsummer. There were no clothes hung out to dry, and no growing crops in sight; but there were small stacks of corn-stalks at different points on the field, and these were in every stage of decay, from the conical heap overgrown with vines to the flat mound of gray stalks through which the young chestnuts had sprouted and grown to a thrifty height. A forest of hop-vines grew over the eaves of the house, flaunting their green tendrils in the soft south wind, and giving an unmistakably home-like air to the place. As no one appeared after an hour's watching, it was more than likely that the family was absent for the day or asleep inside. The longer the soldiers waited, the greater their curiosity became, and then they remembered their scarcity of food, and felt the gold coins in their pockets. It would be foolish to return without buying something from these neighbor-people. Their vow was not to go down from the mountain; and if they neglected this opportunity to supply their wants, starvation would soon drive them into the Confederacy, vow or no vow.

Bromley, as usual, was the first to come to a decision; and then all three climbed boldly out upon the bank and prepared to visit the house. As they advanced over the grass they buttoned their overcoats more closely about their throats, and jingled the coins in their pockets to keep up their courage. They looked down at their bare feet and legs, which naturally made them timid at the prospect of meeting women; and so, huddled together for support, they crossed the dry chip dirt, and came around the corner of the house. The door stood open above the smooth stone step, and Bromley struck it with his knuckles, while his comrades waited behind him, feeling instinctively, in their momentary embarrassment, for their collars and wristbands, which had never before been out of their reach in the presence of the other sex. If they had been less embarrassed they would have noticed the utter absence of all signs of habitation outside the house, and that the door itself was sagging inward from its rusty hinges. The interior was darkened by the sliding boards which closed the windows, and gave forth a musty, earthy smell.

"There's nobody lives here," said Bromley, in his strong, natural voice, at which Coleman and Philip were startled into a small spasm of feeling again for their shirt-collars; and then, as he gave a kick to the lurching door, they dropped their nervous fingers and followed him in. Bromley opened one of the windows, which let in but a dim light because of the thick mat of hop-vines which had overgrown it. The first object that caught the eyes of the soldiers was a considerable library of books crowded together on three shelves above the fireplace.

Philip had his hand at once on the familiar cover of "Uncle Tom's Cabin"; Bromley took down a faded volume of the "Anti-Slavery Record" for the year 1836; and Coleman went outside the door to examine a small book which bore in gilded letters on the cover, "The Branded Hand." On the title-page there was a woodcut of a hand with two S's on the open palm. The story was of the trial and imprisonment of Jonathan Waller, or Walker, at Pensacola, Florida; and a few pages on, the author was shown dripping with perspiration in the pillory. This book had been published in 1845, and Lieutenant Coleman dropped it on the door-step and hastened back to find something more modern. In fact, the three soldiers were moved by the same desire to find something—anything—that had been printed since the year 1864. So it was with the greatest disgust that they took from the lower

THE DESERTED HOUSE.

shelf and threw down, one after another, such ancient history as "Captain Canot; or, Twenty Years of an African Slaver," 1854; "The Alton Riots," by Rev. Edward Beecher, 1838; "Abolition a Sedition," 1839; "Memoir of Rev. Elijah P. Lovejoy," 1838; and "Slavery Unmasked," 1856. There were other curious works on the same subject, bearing equally remote dates.

On the second shelf there was a mixed collection of thin periodicals in blue, yellow, and gray covers, such as "The Quarterly Anti-Slavery Magazine," "The Emancipator," and "The Slave's Friend," and several volumes of speeches by William Lloyd Garrison and Wendell Phillips, bearing date as late as 1858.

The upper shelf was filled with small books and pamphlets on temperance and prohibition, not one of which had been published since the year 1852.

Lieutenant Coleman and Bromley were so keenly disappointed at finding among so many books nothing that threw any light on the state of the country since their arrival on the mountain, that they were almost tempted to throw the library into the fireplace and burn it up by starting a fire with their flints.

The perfect order in which the books had been arranged was strangely in contrast with the otherwise wrecked condition of the room. The excitement of the soldiers on seeing the library had prevented them from noticing that the hearthstone had been wrenched from its original position, and that the earth had been dug out to some depth beneath it and thrown in a heap against the edge of the single bunk by the south wall. Stones had been pried from the back of the chimney, and there was abundant evidence that some person had been hunting for treasure. The rusty spade with which the digging had been done lay in the fireplace, where it had been thrown by the baffled robber. The bedtick had been ripped open with a knife, and the straw with which it had been filled was scattered over the dry earth on the floor. The blankets and everything of value in the house had been carried away. It might be that murder had been committed here as well as robbery. As there was no stain of blood on the mattress or on the floor, Lieutenant Coleman concluded that the robber was only a cowardly thief who had stolen the property from the deserted cabin. It would seem, however, that this man had had some knowledge of the dead mountaineer which had caused him to suspect that there was hidden treasure in the house. Possibly he had found what he sought.

The discovery of the house and its contents was so startling that the soldiers forgot all about the bee-tree they had come in search of. The absence of everything in the nature of food forced itself upon their minds, as they felt the coins in their pockets. There might be corn in one of the tumbledown outhouses. Both were sadly decayed and broken by the winds and storms to which the strong walls and good roof of the house had not yet yielded. The first shed contained a small heap of wood and a rusty ax, and the other appeared to have been used as a cow-stall.

The paths were overgrown with grass, which indicated

that years had passed since the place had been inhabited. The good order in which the books had been left led the soldiers to doubt if the place had been visited since the robber had gone away. It was true that the library was of a character that would be undesirable in a slaveholding Confederacy; and if any one had seen it since the robbery, it was strange that he had not destroyed the objectionable books.

This state of things was so puzzling to Lieutenant Coleman and his comrades that they set out at once to make the circuit of this small tract on the mountain-top, which they naturally believed must be somewhat difficult of access. There must be a road that led to it. The robber might have climbed over the rocks, through some difficult pass, and so might the owner of the house; but the cow-shed would make it seem that domestic animals had been driven up from the valley. The western front was the boulder side of the mountain, and as unapproachable here as on their own plateau. After the most careful exploration, the remaining sides were found to be of the same character as the Cashiers valley side beyond the dividing cliff. This smaller tract of mountain-top was supported by sheer ledges which rose above the forest below. There might be some point in the wall where a man could scale it with the help of a long ladder, but it was evident that no cow had ever fed in that stall.

It was past noon now, and the soldiers sat down on a rock in the mild sunlight which poured over the dividing ledge, and talked of the strange situation.

"There have been human beings here," said Bromley; "at least two of them: the fellow who lived in that house, and the robber who looted it. Now I am not much of a detective, but it is certainly our business to find out how they got here and how they got away."

"How the robber got away," suggested Coleman; "for there is no doubt in my mind that the man who lived here was his victim."

"Yes," said Philip, "I am certain there was a murder committed here. Don't you see that if the murderer had carried off the books they would have been evidence against him sufficient to have convicted him of the crime?"

This view of Philip's was so plausible that the others adopted it. They assumed that the unfortunate victim had been shot in the open field, and buried where he fell. If the crime had been committed so long ago that the grass had found time to take root in the hard paths, it would have long since overgrown the shallow grave. Then it occurred to the soldiers, who had helped to bury the dead on more than one battle-field, that as time passes a shallow grave has a way of sinking. The murderer would have been careful not to raise a mound, and the very place of his crime should by this time be plainly marked by a long grassy hollow.

They started at once to search for the grave; but they were thirsty, not to say hungry, after their exertions of the morning, and so they went first to a spring which they had seen near the head of the path where they had climbed up. It was a large bubbling spring, and flowed under the rocks so nearly opposite to where the branch appeared on the other side that they knew it was the source of their own supply. It was not pleasant to think how easily their neighbor in his lifetime might have turned it in some other direction, thus stopping the wheels of their mill, and possibly leaving them to perish of thirst.

After they had lain down on the ground and drunk from the spring, they turned in the direction of the lonely house, flattering themselves that they were, after all, pretty clever detectives. By putting together the facts which they had now determined and proved, they had made a rather shrewd beginning at the discovery of a crime. They agreed, as they went along, that nothing further should be disturbed within or without the house until they should have unraveled the history of the foul murder. That was, they believed, the method observed by the best detectives and coroners. They might not establish their theory to-day or to-morrow, but they could go and come by the new path they had found, and sooner or later they would force the secret from the mute objects in the midst of which the crime had been committed.

As they arrived at this united and enthusiastic decision, they were approaching the house on the opposite side to that which they had passed on their first coming. The turf was so firmly rooted here that it was not easy to determine whether there had or had not been a garden on this side. A thick clump of young chestnut-trees had grown up since cultivation had been suspended, and as the three soldiers turned around these, they came suddenly upon something which exploded their fine-spun theories.

It was nothing less than a grave with an uncommonly high mound above it, and marked at the head by a broad slab of oak. Besides the wild-rose bush which grew out of the matted grass on the mound, there was another object which staggered the soldiers more than the grave itself. On the upper part of the headboard the following inscription was deeply cut:

HERE
REST THE BONES
OF
HEZEKIAH WALLSTOW
ABOLITIONIST
AND
APOSTLE OF TEMPERANCE
WHO DIED

Here ended the letters, which were cut with a knife, evidently by the said Hezekiah himself, with the expenditure of much time and patience. Below, the inscription was continued with black paint, half written and half printed in one ungrammatical and badly spelled sentence:

Hit was sumwhar betune
April 26 & Juin the 4,
1858.

The other object, found lying across the grave, was the skeleton of the cow, whose crumpled horns were attached

THE GRAVE OF THE OLD MAN OF THE MOUNTAIN.

to the bleached skull, and whose white ribs provided a trellis for the rose-bush. Strangest of all strange things in this mysterious affair, one horn of the skeleton was hooked over the top of the slab so as to hold the great skull reversed close against the headboard on the side opposite to the inscription. Evidently the faithful creature had died of starvation during the winter which followed the death of her master. By accident or through a singular exhibition of affection, she had lain down to die on the hard snow which was banked high above the grave, and as this melted the head of the cow had lodged in this remarkable position.

"Well," said Philip, with a sigh for his pet theory, "whoever he was and however he came here, his name was Hezekiah Wallstow, and there was no murder after all—unless a third man came to bury him."

"That's all settled," said Bromley, resignedly; "but how about the cow? Did she come here in a balloon?"

"My dear fellow," said Lieutenant Coleman, "we have not yet found how the men got here. When we learn that, it may make all the rest plain."

Without entering the house again, the soldiers made a second circuit of the field, examining carefully every foot of the cliffs. They were absolutely certain now that there was no road or path leading to this smaller plateau except that by which they themselves had come; and yet here were the bones of a full-grown cow and the ruined stall which had at some time been her winter quarters. They next examined the heaps of stalks, which were sixteen in number, and represented that many harvests; but the older ones were little more than a thin layer of decayed litter through which the grass and bushes had grown up. There might have been many others of an earlier date, all traces of which had long since disappeared. At first it seemed strange that a cow should have starved in the deepest snow in the midst of such surroundings. On a closer examination, however, it appeared that the tops of the two larger stacks had been much torn, and the stiff stalks cropped bare of leaves. It was plain enough that the lean cow had wandered here on the hard crust of the snow and scattered the stalks as she fed. Even now these could be seen lying all about in the grass where they had lodged when the snow melted. Under one of the stacks another skull was found, the owner of which must have died before the cow, or have been killed for beef. Instead of one, two domestic animals, then, had cropped the grass and switched at the flies on this plateau which was surrounded by inaccessible cliffs. How did they come there?

By sunset the soldiers were no nearer to a solution of this difficult problem, and so they filled their two pails with antislavery books, and returned to ponder and wonder in the society of the bear and the six sad roosters.

They could sleep but little after such a day of excitement, and they were scarcely refreshed by their night's rest when they returned on the following day to the deserted house. This time they left their overcoats at home, and took with them a loaf of corn-bread for luncheon, and the pails, in which they intended to bring back more books.

They halted again before the oak slab bearing the name of Hezekiah Wallstow, apostle of temperance, etc., and crowned by the mourning skull of the cow, as if to assure themselves of the reality of what they had seen, and then they walked humbly into the house. They could think of no guiding clue to start them in the solution of the problem of the cattle, and so they weakly yielded to their curiosity about the books. Bromley cut away the thicket of hop-vines which darkened the two windows, and in the improved light they fell to examining the coarse woodcuts of runaway slaves with their small belongings tied up in a pocket-handkerchief, which headed certain advertisements in the periodicals. "The Adventures of Captain Canot" was a thick book with numerous illustrations of a distressing character. In one picture a jolly sailor with a pipe in his mouth was smilingly branding the back of an African woman, while another sailor stood by with a lantern in broad daylight. They hoped to find an account-book or a diary, but there was nothing of the sort on the shelves beyond one or two entries in pencil on a fly-leaf of the "Memoir of Rev. Elijah P. Lovejoy," acknowledging the receipt of a cask of meal or a quarter of lamb.

CHAPTER XXIII

STARVATION

FOLLOWING their first visit, the three soldiers returned during four successive days to the deserted house and the field surrounding it. By this time they had carried home the last of the books by pailfuls, making the long journey through the cave of the bats by torch-light; but they had arrived no nearer to the solution of the riddle of the cattle. In fact, so long as any part of the library remained where they had found it, they had come to wander hopelessly in the early morning along the ledges which upheld the smaller plateau, and then retire to the cool house to read.

After the books had been removed by the soldiers to their own side of the dividing cliff, they found it so hard to leave them that they stopped at home for a whole week, reading by turns and worrying themselves thin about the bones of the cattle. They had abundant need at this time to keep their flesh and spirits, for two more of the nine sacks of corn had been ground in the mill, and the prospect for the future was more dismal than ever. The end of this week of inaction, however, found the three soldiers in the early morning again standing by the deserted house.

Lieutenant Coleman had a systematic, military mind, and, now the diverting books were out of their reach, he stated the problem to his companions in this direct and concise way:

"We know that two cattle have lived and died on this field."

"Undoubtedly," replied Bromley and Philip.

"We have examined three sides of the field, and found that the cattle could not have come from either of those directions. Is not that so?"

"It is absolutely certain," said the others.

"Therefore," continued Lieutenant Coleman, "they must have come by the fourth side."

This conclusion was admitted to be logical; but it provoked a storm of argument, in the course of which the soldiers got wild-eyed and red in the face. In the end, however, they consented to trim out the bushes which formed a thicket along the base of the ledge. It seemed to Lieutenant Coleman that they must find some passage here, and, sure enough, not far from the middle of this natural wall they came upon a low-browed opening, which presently narrowed down to a space not much more than five feet square. The farther end of this tunnel was closed by a pile of loose earth, which was spread out at the base, and had every appearance of having been thrown in from the other side of the ledge. The rusty shovel was brought from the fireplace of the house, and after a few minutes of vigorous digging, a ray of light broke through the roots and grass near the roof of the hole. The soldiers gave a wild cheer, and rushed out into the fresh air to cool off.

"That settles it," said Lieutenant Coleman. "Hezekiah Wallstow was the old man of the mountain, and after Josiah Woodring buried him he filled up this passage. The treasure he was searching for was the very cask of gold we dug out of the fake grave—thanks to the sacrilegious behavior of the bear."

"But how about the cattle?" said Bromley, still skeptical.

"Easy enough," said Coleman, triumphantly. "They brought two young calves up the ladders."

This hitherto unsuspected passage through the ledge made everything clear. It had evidently been wide open during all the years the old man had lived on the mountain. It might have been screened by bushes so that any chance visitors, like the hunters who came over the bridge, would be easily deceived, and not disposed to look farther than the ruined cabin and the non-committal gravestone.

It was not strange that the three soldiers had never suspected that there was an opening here through the rocks, for a four-pronged chestnut had taken firm root in the grassy bank which Josiah had thrown up, and the old man had been dead six years when they first arrived on the mountain. How soon after the burial the passageway had been closed, it was not so easy to determine, but numerous hollows which were afterward found near certain trees and rocks on the smaller plateau made it look as if Josiah had spent a good many moonlight nights in digging for the treasure before he gave it up altogether. According to the story of Andy, the guide, Josiah himself must have died soon after his strange patron, and most likely he closed the entrance to the passage in despair when he felt his last illness approaching. There was still much for the soldiers to learn about the motive of the hermit in burying his surplus gold. The comforts with which he had surrounded himself would indicate that he was no miser, and his devotion to the cause of the slave made it extremely probable that he had willed his treasure to some emancipation society, which had not succeeded in reclaiming it before the war, and which, for plenty of reasons, had not been able to secure it since.

After the soldiers had reopened the passage through the dividing cliff so that they could pass readily from one plateau to the other, they suspended further investigation and yielded to the luxury of reading, which had been denied them so long. The more they read of this peculiar literature from the library left by Hezekiah Wallstow, the more interested they became in the cause of the slave who, they believed, had been made free on paper by the impotent proclamation of Abraham Lincoln, only to have his fetters more firmly riveted than ever by the success of the Confederate arms.

Among the other books there was one entitled "Twofold Slavery of the United States." This book had been published in London in the year 1854, and contained as a frontispiece a black-and-white map, which, so far west as it extended, was remarkably like the one which hung on the wall of their house. Philip shed new tears over the pathetic lives of Uncle Tom and little Eva, and Lieutenant Coleman and George Bromley grew more and more indignant as they read of the sufferings of the Rev. Elijah P. Lovejoy, and the self-confessed cruelties of Captain Carnot. However much the soldiers were wrought up by these books, it was left to the mass of pamphlets and periodicals to fill their hearts with an unspeakable bitterness toward the institution which the united efforts of their comrades in arms had failed to overthrow.

It was evident that the old man had kept up some sort of communication by mail with the Boston abolitionists, and that his agent, Josiah, had yielded his views, if he had any, to a liberal supply of gold; for up to the time of his death he had continued to receive these periodicals. As long as he received such dangerous publications, he must have maintained correspondence with their editors; and the more the soldiers became imbued by their reading with the ideas which had made a hermit of Hezekiah Wallstow, the more certain they became that he had willed his money to the cause of abolition, or perhaps that he only held it in trust from the first. Otherwise, why should he have adopted so crafty a method of hiding it from Josiah? To speculate on the cunning of these two men became a favorite occupation of Coleman and Bromley when their eyes were worn out with reading. They were sure that every fresh lot of pamphlets had come, through the settlement and up the mountain, at the bottom of a cask of meal.

The old man had no mill or other means of grinding his corn, which he must have cultivated for his cattle, relying upon Josiah for most of his food. Undoubtedly the very keg which the hunters had seen Josiah carrying up by moonlight, and which they believed was filled with whisky, contained seditious literature enough, if they had ever found it, to have put them to the unpleasant necessity of hanging the bearer to the nearest limb.

So the soldiers continued to read, to the neglect of every other duty, through the entire month of August, except that Lieutenant Coleman made a brief entry in the diary each morning, and, when they were out of food, Philip laid by his book long enough to grind another sack of the corn. The few ears which had shown themselves on the plantation had been eaten green, and the yellow and shriveled stalks which had escaped the grub at the root stood in thin, sickly rows. It was an off year even for the chestnuts. When, in addition to this, it was found in September that the potato crop had rotted in the ground, the reading was brought to a sudden end, and the soldiers found themselves face to face with a condition which threatened starvation, and that before the winter began. They remembered the bee-tree, and took up the line where Philip had left it, at the edge of the southern wall, only to find that the bees flew on to some tree in the forest below and beyond the plateau.

When it was quite settled that they would have no supplies for the winter unless they bought them from the people in the valley with their gold pieces, as the old man had done before them, they settled down to their reading again, foraging by turns for every edible thing they could find, and putting off the evil hour when they should be forced to reveal themselves. The more they read of these fiery periodicals the more they loathed their neighbors in the valley and shrank from communicating with them. They knew that these people in the mountains seldom owned slaves themselves; but they felt that they were in full sympathy with all the cruelties of which the yellow-and-blue covered pamphlets treated. If the guineas in the hoard of Hezekiah Wallstow meant anything, they represented the proportion of the gold which had been contributed by antislavery societies in England; and they began seriously to consider their moral obligation to return the entire sum to its rightful owners. In order to accomplish this just purpose, their lives must be preserved during the approaching winter, and seeds secured for another planting. After that, they would find means to replace with iron the gold they had used in the construction of the mill and of various domestic utensils; and when the treasure was restored to the cask, they would find some way to open communication with the benevolent antislavery societies.

By the end of October they had eaten the last of their meal. There were a few clusters of purple grapes on the vines, and to these they turned for food, still dreading to make any signs to their enemies, with a dread which was born of the pamphlets they were reading. For two days more they stained their hands and faces with the juice of the grapes, until an exclusive fruit diet, and meditation day and night on the awful wickedness of men, weakened their bodies and began to affect their minds.

The dread hour had finally come, and they could no longer delay making signs of their distress. To this end they collected a pile of dry wood, and heaped it on the point of rocks, in full view of the settlement of Cashiers. It was growing dusk when everything was ready to start the fire, and Philip had come from the house with a lighted torch. At the moment he was about to touch it to the dry wood, Bromley snatched the torch from his hand and extinguished it in the dirt. Coleman and Philip tried to prevent this rash act of their comrade, and in their excitement gave free expression to their anger; but Bromley stamped out the last spark of the fire without paying any heed to their bad language and frantic gestures.

"Are you mad?" he then cried, retreating a little from what threatened to be an assault. "What do you think will be our fate at the hands of these people, when we are found in possession of such books as we have been reading? We should be imprisoned like Lovejoy, or branded like Walker. We might pay with our lives for your recklessness to-night."

Philip and Coleman were shocked at the danger they had so narrowly escaped, and thanked Bromley for his forethought and prompt action.

Of course they must bury the books, but they would have all of the next day to attend to that; and with many expressions of thankfulness they returned to the house and crept into their bunks. When morning came they were weak and hungry, with nothing whatever to eat; but in spite of all this they heaped the antislavery books and pamphlets on the earthen floor, carefully separating them from the works on temperance. They had come to regard these books as little less than sacred, and they naturally shrank from burying them in the ground. Happy thought! —there was the cave of the bats. So, packing them into the pails, the soldiers carried the books in two toilsome journeys by torch-light to the middle of the cavernous passage, and laid them carefully together on the stone floor. They were well-nigh exhausted by this exertion; but after a rest they found strength to close the entrance with brush and earth, and to cover their work with pine-needles.

Half famished as Lieutenant Coleman and his comrades were, they could only drink from the branch and wait patiently for night. The poor old paralyzed rooster, sitting in the chips by the door, looked so forlorn and hungry that Philip set him out among the dry weeds, and lay down on the ground beside him, so as to be ready to turn him about and set him along when he had plucked the few seeds in his front. As for the bear and the five crippled roosters, they shambled and hobbled about, and shifted bravely for themselves.

There were still many things to consider as to how they would be received by these people, and what success they would have in exchanging United States gold pieces for food and clothing. Perhaps they would be obliged to buy Confederate notes at ruinous rates of exchange. Perhaps their visitors would confiscate their gold pieces at sight,

THE BEACON FIRE.

and take them down the mountain as State prisoners. They must keep some coins in their pockets for barter, which was their object in summoning their dubious neighbors; but it would certainly be prudent to conceal the bulk of their money. So the last thing the soldiers did on this November afternoon was to dump the gold that remained in the cask into a hole in the ground, and cover it up.

As soon as it began to grow dark on the mountain they set fire to the pile of wood, which was presently a great tower of flame, lighting up the rocks and trees, and forming a beacon which must be seen from valley and mountain for miles around. At that hour, and in the glare of their own fire, they could see nothing of its effect in the settlement; but they were sure it would be watched by the families outside every cabin; and in this belief they moved about to the right and left of the flames, waving their arms in token of their distress.

Surely a fire on this mountain-top, where no native had set foot for seven long years, would excite the wonder of the people below. It could be kindled only by human hands, and they would be eager to know to whom the hands belonged.

In the morning the three soldiers crept out to the smoldering remains of their fire, which was still sending up a thin wreath of smoke. On the distant road through the valley they could see groups of tiny people, evidently watching and wondering. They could come no nearer than the bridgeless gorge, and so, weak as the soldiers were, after making every effort to show themselves in the smoke, they made their way to the head of the ladders and climbed down to the field below. Philip stopped behind to run up the old flag on the pole; for, whatever effect that emblem might have on their neighbors, they were determined to stand by their colors. They found a few chestnuts and dried berries in the old field, which they devoured with wolfish hunger as they crept along toward the gorge.

They hoped to see human faces on the opposite bank when they arrived; but there was no one there to meet them. They were not greatly disappointed, for it was still early in the day, and the people had a much longer journey to make from the valley. There was the same old-time stillness on that part of the mountain: the tinkling brook in the bottom of the gorge, and the soughing of the wind in the tops of the tall pines on the other side. There were still some sticks of the old bridge wedged in the top of the dead basswood—the bridge which had served the old abolitionist in his lifetime, and the destruction of which had served the purpose of the soldiers equally well.

The mild November sunshine lay bright on the faded landscape, and the soldiers sat down on the dry grass to await the coming of their deliverers. If one of the tall pines had been standing on their own side of the gorge they would have used their last strength to cut it down and fell it across the chasm. They had put on their old blue overcoats, to make a decent appearance before the people when they arrived; but hour after hour crept slowly by, and nobody came except Tumbler, the bear, who had backed down the ladders and shambled across the field to join them. By the sun it was past noon when he came, and as he seated himself silently in the gloomy circle, he made but a sorry addition to the anxious waiters. Why did no one come to their relief? They knew that their fire had been seen where the presence of a human being would be regarded as little less than a miracle by the dwellers in the valley. What if they had accepted it as a miracle altogether, and avoided the place accordingly? They were ignorant people, and therefore superstitious; or else they were as cruel and heartless as they were described in the "Weekly Emancipator."

The rustling wind in the tree-tops, and the occasional tapping of a woodpecker in the forest beyond, became hateful sounds to their impatient ears. Bromley, who was the strongest of the three, and the more indignant that no one came to their relief, wandered back upon the old field, where he found a few more chestnuts, which he divided equally with his half-famished comrades. Every mouthful of food helped to keep up their strength and courage, and now the slanting rays of the afternoon sun reminded them that they must repeat their signal, and that no time was to be lost in gathering wood for another fire. There was still hope that relief would come before dark, and Philip was left to watch with the bear, while Coleman and Bromley returned to the plateau.

The postmaster in the Cove might be less superstitious, they thought, or less hard-hearted than the people in the valley. If their strength held out they would have two fires that night. No chance should be neglected. As Coleman and Bromley dragged together a few dead limbs upon the edge of the great boulder, they hoped that the postmaster had found the remains of the telescope, as they knew he had found the army blanket which fell from the balloon, so that when he saw their fire he would connect it, in his mind, with the other objects which had come down from the mountain.

It was after sunset when Philip and Tumbler appeared on the plateau. No one had come even so far as the gorge; and Philip helped to carry the last of their wood to the rocky point where the blackened embers of the first fire lay in the thin ashes. Coleman and Philip remained to kindle this beacon, while Bromley went to the Cove side with a lighted torch and a bundle of fat pine-knots. When Bromley saw the first smoke of the other fire across the ridge, no light had yet appeared in the windows of the small post-office. Moreover, with his strong eyes he was sure he saw some object moving along the road in the direction of the office. He waited a little, waving his torch, and then he applied it to the dry leaves and sticks at the base of the pile, which flashed quickly into a blaze. Bromley was not content to move about in the light replenishing his fire, but, as often as a fat pine-knot had become enveloped in flame, he separated it from the pile and poked it over the edge of the great smooth rock, to flare against the black storm-stains as it fell, and perhaps to start a new fire in the Cove bottom. A brisk east wind was blowing across the mountain, which carried the smoke and sparks over the long roof of the post-office. Bromley remained late at his work; but at last his strength and his will-power yielded to the weakness that comes with hunger. An overpowering drowsiness compelled him to leave the fire and go stumbling over the hill to the house, where he found Coleman and Philip already asleep.

CHAPTER XXIV

THE RESCUE

WHEN the three soldiers awoke on the morning which followed the kindling of the two fires, Philip was too ill to leave his bunk, and Lieutenant Coleman and Bromley were too weak to drag themselves as far as the rocks where the embers were still smoking. The sun was shining on their United States window, and when they looked out at the door, the old flag of thirty-five stars was floating bravely on the fresh wind.

"Three cheers for the stars and stripes, and for Sherman Territory!" cried Bromley, and the weak cheers so exhausted the two men that they sat down on the wooden bench in a state of collapse. Faint as they were from hunger, they were still fainter from thirst, and after a moment's rest they staggered over to the branch and drank their fill of the cool water, and laved their feverish faces in the stream. They brought a cup of the water to Philip, who lay quietly in his bunk, and was altogether so weak that they were obliged to hold him up while he drank.

"There, there," said Coleman, as they eased him back

on his pillow. "You must keep a good heart, for some one will surely come to us to-day."

Philip looked brighter for the draft of water, but he only smiled in reply. The sun was warm outside, but the act of drinking, while it had greatly revived and encouraged Coleman and Bromley, had so chilled their starved bodies that they put on their overcoats and buttoned them up to the throat. They could do no more in the way of calling for help than they had already done. Men had died of starvation before, and it might be their fate to perish of hunger, but they had a strong faith that the fires they had built for two nights on this uninhabited mountain would bring some one to their relief. They regretted now that the reading of the abolition books had influenced them to delay so long their appeal for help. To reach them their rescuers must fell one or more of the tall pines across the bridgeless gorge, but they were too weak to go down the ladders, and what wind there was blew across the mountain in the direction of the gorge, so that they would not be able to hear the sound of an ax a mile away. Time had never dragged so slowly before. The sun lay in at the open door, and by the marks they had made on the floor, as well as by the shadows cast by the trees outside, they could judge closely of the hour. They could hardly believe that it was only ten o'clock in the morning, when it seemed as if they had already passed a whole day in vain hope of relief.

It was such a terrible thing to await starvation in the oppressive stillness of the mountain, that Bromley, almost desperate with listening, went to the branch and hung the bucket on the arm of the old Slow-John, which presently began to pound and splash in its measured way. Dismal as the sound was, it gave them something to count, and relieved their tired ears of the monotonous flapping of the flag and of the rustling of the barren corn-stalks.

They talked of the old man who had died alone on the other plateau. He, too, might have died of starvation. There were no signs of food in the deserted house when they had discovered it. They had never thought of it before, but his cunning agent might have been a villain after all. He might have grown weary at last of lugging casks up the mountain by moonlight, and getting the old man's gold by slow doles. He must have had some knowledge of the treasure for which he dug so persistently afterward, and in his greed to possess it he might have deliberately starved the old abolitionist. They thought of Hezekiah Wallstow burning beacon-fires in his extremity, when there was a good bridge to connect the mountain-top with the valley, and yet he was left to die alone. The thought was not encouraging to Coleman and Bromley in their weakened, nervous condition, and tended to make them more than ever distrustful of the natives to whom they had appealed.

They withheld these disturbing suspicions from Philip, but the more they pondered on the subject the more they were convinced of the barbarity of the Confederates, and of their determination to leave them to their fate.

Lieutenant Coleman wrote what he believed to be the last entry in the diary. It was November 7, 1871; and on the prepared paper of the book which treated of deep-sea fishing, he stated briefly their starving condition and their fruitless efforts to summon relief. They still had the tin box in which the adamantine candles had been stored, and into this Bromley helped to pack the leaves of the diary, already neatly tied in separate packages, and labeled for each year. If he had had a little more strength he would have carried it to the forge, and sealed the cover of the box which contained the record of their lives. As it was, they set it on the mantelpiece under the trophy formed of the station flags and the swords and carbines, and laid a weight on the lid.

After this was accomplished, Lieutenant Coleman lay down and turned his face to the wall, and Bromley seated himself on the bench outside the door, too stubborn to give up all hope of relief. The warm sun lighted the chip dirt at his feet, and seemed to glorify the bright colors of the old flag as it floated from the staff. He forgot his desperate situation for a moment, as his mind turned back to the battle-days when he had seen it waving in the sulphurous smoke. It gave him no comfort, however, to think of his old comrades and the dead generals and the cause that was lost; and when his eyes fell on the ground at his feet, he tried to keep them fixed on a tiny ant which came out of a crumbling log. The small thing was so full of life, darting and halting and turning this way and that! Now it disappeared under the log, and then it came out again, rolling a kernel of corn by climbing up on one side of the grain, to fall ignominiously down on the other. Bromley was just about to pounce on the grain of corn and crush it between his teeth when he heard a sound on the hill, and, raising his eyes, he saw two men coming on toward the house. They carried long bird-rifles on their shoulders, and to his starved vision they looked to be of gigantic size against the sky.

He could only cry out, "Fred! Fred! Here they come!"

These electric words brought Coleman's haggard face to the door, and even Philip turned in his blankets.

The strange dress and wild appearance of the two soldiers clinging to the door of the house, and the fantastic effect of the afternoon sun on the stained-glass window, as if the interior were on fire, so startled the strangers that they lowered their rifles to a position for defense, and turned from the direct approach, until they had gained a position among the rustling corn-stalks in front of the door. The various buildings and the evidence of cultivation on the mountain-top staggered the visitors, and the haggard faces of Coleman and Bromley led them to believe that they had come upon a camp of the fabled wild men of the woods. They had never seen a stained-glass window before, and to their minds it suggested some infernal magic, so the two valley-men stood elbow to elbow in an attitude for defense, and waited for the others to speak.

"Come on, neighbors," said Bromley, holding out his empty hands. "We are only three starving men."

One of the valley-men was tall and lank, and the other was sturdily built; and at these pacific words of Bromley they advanced, still keeping close together.

"HE COULD ONLY CRY OUT, 'FRED! FRED! HERE THEY COME!'"

"We don't see but two," said the stout man, coming to a halt again. "Where's the other one at?"

"He's too weak to get out of his bunk," said Lieutenant Coleman. "For God's sake, have you brought us food?"

"That's just what we have," said the rosy-faced stout man, who came on without any further hesitation. "We've brought ye a corn-pone. We 'lowed there might be some human critters starvin' up here." With that he whisked about the thin man, and snatched a corn-loaf from the haversack on his back.

"How did you-all ever git here?" said the thin man. "Hit's seven year since the old bridge tumbled into the gorge."

There was no reply to this question, for Bromley was devouring his bread like a starved wolf, while Coleman had turned away to share his piece with Philip.

The eagerness with which they ate seemed to please the two valley-men, who were willing enough to wait a reasonable time for the information they sought. It was a fine opportunity to give some account of themselves, and the rosy-faced man made good use of it.

"We're plumb friendly," he said, "and mighty glad we brought along the bread, ain't we, Tom? Might n't 'a' done hit if hit had n't 'a' been for my old woman insistin'. She 'lowed some hunter fellers had got up here and could n't git down ag'in, and she hild fast to that idea while she was a-bakin' last night, time your fire was a-burnin'. Hit certainly takes women folks to git the rights o' things, don't hit, Tom? My name is Riley Hooper, and this yer friend o' mine is Tom Zachary, and we 're nothin' if we ain't friendly."

Poor Philip was unable to swallow the dry bread, and Coleman came to the door with the golden cup in his hand, and begged one of the men to bring a cup of water from the branch. Tom Zachary hurried off on this mission of mercy.

"Hit 's a wonder," he exclaimed, when he came back with the dripping cup, "that you-all ain't been pizoned afore this, drinkin' out o' brass gourds. That 's what ailed Colum. Long time he had the greensickness. But his woman was cookin' into a brass kittle, and that might 'a' made some difference."

The two men now pressed into the house to see Philip, and Bromley, whose hands were at last empty, and whose strength was fast returning, came after them.

"I 'm jist nacherly put out," said Hooper, when he saw the condition of Philip, "that I did n't bring along somethin' to warm up a cold stomic. Poor feller! Say, where 's your fryin'-pan at? I 'll fix a dose for him. Here, Tom, wake up. Fill this skillet with water out o' the branch, 'thout no flavor o' brass into hit"; and as he spoke he whisked Tom around again, and took the haversack from his shoulders. "No, ye don't," said he to Bromley, who came forward for more bread. "No, ye don't, my boy. I 've viewed starvin' humans afore. What you want to do is to go slow. A dose o' gruel is jest the ticket for this yer whole outfit."

The rosy-faced man was too busy with the fire and the gruel, and too eager to improve the condition of the men he had rescued, to ask any disturbing questions; and Tom Zachary was so considerate, in the presence of actual starvation, that he seated himself on a three-legged stool, and stared at the stained-glass windows and the flags and the curious map on the wall. It was just as well that Bromley had removed the golden casters, years before, from the legs of the stools, when they were found to make ruts and furrows in the earthen floor. Tom Zachary would have been more astonished than ever if he had found himself rolling about on double-eagles.

When the hot gruel had been served, Philip was so much revived as to be able to sit up on the edge of his bunk. If it was delicacy that still prevented the visitors from asking questions, it was a dread of overwhelming bad news that sealed the soldiers' lips. They had become so settled in their convictions, and so confirmed in their strange blindness, that they shrank from hearing the mortifying particulars. So the five men sat staring at one another, each party waiting for the other to begin.

"Sojer coats," said the lean man, nudging his companion.

"And cavalry guns and swords," said the rosy-faced one, casting his eyes on the trophy.

"And my affydavid," said the tall one, "if them ain't the reg'lar old signal-flags—one, two, one."

Lieutenant Coleman was thankful that his visitors had said nothing disagreeable thus far, but he feared every moment that they would make some insulting remark about the old flag, which they could see through the doorway.

Bromley restrained himself as long as he could, and then, in reply to the three mild observations, in which he thought he detected a shade of sarcasm, he exclaimed:

"Well, what of it? We are not ashamed of our uniform or of our arms."

"There ain't no reason why ye should be, my buck," said the rosy-faced man. "Soldierin' is as good a trade as any other."

"Hit 's better 'n some," said the tall one.

"Gentlemen," said Lieutenant Coleman, who began to fear more personal remarks, "you have saved our lives to-day. We shall never forget your kindness, or cease to feel ourselves your debtors. You see our destitute condition. We need food for the coming winter, and seed for another year, for which we are able to pay; and if you know who owns this mountain-top, we shall be glad to arrange, through you, to buy it."

"Well, now, I 'll be gormed," said the rosy-faced man, "if he ain't a thoroughbred as soon 's he gits fed up a little. Wants to buy these yer rocks, does he? Tom, who do you reckon owns this mounting?"

"Dunno," said Tom, with a grin, "if you don't."

"Well, I do," said Hooper, expanding himself with an air of proprietorship, "and there hain't nobody never disputed my title to this upper kentry."

"Are you willing to sell it?" said Lieutenant Coleman.

"I'll sell anything I've got," said Hooper, looking more rosy and smiling than ever, "so I git my figger."

"Very well," said Coleman. "If we take the mountain-top from the deep gorge up, at what price would you value it?"

"Well, now," said Hooper, "if you really mean business, this yer track ain't worth a fortun'. Timber-land in these parts brings a dollar an acre when hit brings anything. Rock-land like this, without no timber onto hit, is worth fifty cents; but, considerin' the improvements and the buildin's," he continued, "I reckon seventy-five would be dirt-cheap. Hit ain't ever been surveyed, but I 'low there's two hundred acres above the gorge."

Lieutenant Coleman already had his hand in the pocket of his canvas trousers, and, bringing out two double-eagles, he handed them to the rosy-faced proprietor as a first payment. Hooper jumped up from his seat and took the two yellow coins in his hands, and chinked them together, and tossed them about as if he feared they might burn his palms.

"Durned if hit ain't United States gold money, Tom," he exclaimed, passing one of the coins to Zachary, who was equally excited. "We hain't viewed that kind o' money for seven years in these parts, have we, Tom?"

Tom indorsed his companion's statement in pretty strong language, and Lieutenant Coleman hastened to say that if the money was not satisfactory, they could probably agree upon some rate of exchange. At this point of the conversation, the two mountaineers exchanged some words in a whisper, and the soldiers believed they were agreeing upon the discount between United States and Confederate money. To fill up this awkward break in the conversation, Lieutenant Coleman began again to express his gratitude to his rescuers.

"Now, hold on, captain," exclaimed Hooper, facing about. "Whatsoever me and Tom has done, we have done willin', and nobody willin'er, and we're goin' to stand by ye to the end; but we ain't goin' no further in this business till you tell us how ye got here. The way we study hit out, you ain't treatin' me and Tom fair."

"Pardon me, my good friends," said Lieutenant Coleman. "I had no intention of being rude. We came here in the summer of 1864, in the line of our duty as Union soldiers, and when the war ended with the success of the Confederates—"

"What!" cried the two men together, gasping in amazement at what they heard. "And the Union was destroyed," continued Lieutenant Coleman. "And the Capitol fell into the hands of the Confederates." "And slavery was restored," exclaimed Bromley. "And the flag was disgraced and robbed of its stars," put in Philip, with such voice as he could command.

The two mountaineers stood open-mouthed for a moment, and then they burst into peals of laughter. "Whoop!" cried the rosy-faced man, slapping his leg and throwing his wool hat on the floor as if it had been a brickbat. "If that ain't the jolliest thing I ever heard, and hit 's kind o' serious-like, too! Why, men, there ain't no Confederacy. Hit 's the old United States, from Canada to the Gulf of Mexico, and from the Atlantic Ocean clear across to the Pacific."

"And General Sherman—" gasped Philip.

"He 's gineral of the army up in Washington right now, and Gineral Grant is President," cried the rosy-faced man.

Somehow the interior of the house grew vague and misty, as if a sea-fog had swept in through the windows. Everything and everybody danced and reeled about, until the soldiers fell away from the embrace of their deliverers, quite exhausted by the excitement and the news they had heard.

While all this was going on, Philip lay back on his blanket and shed tears of joy over the wonderful news. In fact, there was n't a dry eye in the room. Even the eyes of the men from Cashiers glistened with moisture, as they vied with each other in discharging facts, like cannon-balls, into the ears of the astonished soldiers. They gave them a rough history of the end of the great war, of the tragic death of Lincoln, and of some of the events which had since taken place in the United States.

"There were thirty-five stars on the old flag when we came here," cried Lieutenant Coleman.

"And there 's thirty-seven now," said Hooper.

"Thirty-seven!" repeated the soldiers, looking at one another through their tears. "Thirty-seven!"

The soldiers ate some more of the bread from the haversack, and with renewed strength went out into the afternoon sunlight, Coleman and Bromley supporting Philip, and all five sat down under the old flag. And as they sat there together like brothers, the soldiers told the others why they had first come to the mountain, and the bad news they had got by flag, and the resolution they had made, and all that had come of it. And when they had done speaking, Tom Zachary, whose face had grown longer and sadder as he listened to their story, said he had something to tell them for which he hoped they would forgive him.

"I was only a boy in the war-time," said Tom, "and I lived with my kin-folks in a settlement at the foot of the tenth mountain. Gineral Thomas commanded the Home Guard brigade, with headquarters at Quallatown, in the Cherokee kentry, and he had signal-flag men like you-all, and 'mongst the rest there was one named Bud Bryson. Now Bud was mighty peart, and he boasted as how he could study out any cipher that ever was made, if only he had time enough. So when the gineral heard that there was a Yankee station on that mountain, he sent Bud with a spy-glass, to make out the cipher and read the telegrafts for him. Many's the day I stayed out on the South Ridge with Bud, and wrote down the letters as he read 'em off, and, turn 'em which way we would, we could never make head or tail of 'em. It was a-z-q-j-g and such fool letters, and after two weeks' hard work Bud Bryson was no nearer to makin' sense of the letters than when he begun, though he did always say that if they had only give him time he would 'a' studied out the trick.

"But the gineral got tired o' waitin' on Bud, and one day he sent a squad of fifteen cavalry soldiers to capture the stations. The soldiers started up the mountain in the early mornin', with Bud to guide 'em and give 'em points. I went up with the rest, just to see the fun, and when we got to the top, the soldiers rushed in on two sets o' men, sawin' the air with their flags and sendin' messages both ways. Lieutenant Swann was the officer's name, a big red man, and mighty mad he was when the soldiers took him. They searched him from head to foot, and 'mongst the papers on him they found the secret cipher Bud had been workin' for.

"What with guardin' the prisoners and the prospect of capturin' more, fifteen troopers was too scant a crowd to divide into two squads, and so the captain ordered Bud to stay on the mountain and give the stations ahead enough news to keep 'em quiet until he come back.

"That game suited Bud mighty well, and havin' nobody to help him, he made me stay with him to take down the letters. We had the camp just as they left it, with plenty o' rations and coffee to drink such as we had n't tasted for years, and every time Bud looked at the flags he burst out laughin'. Hit was somewhere near the end of July when we took the mountain, and that same afternoon Bud begun to figger the letters of his first message crooked accordin' to the cipher, and git hit ready to send on. 'Tom,' he says to me with a grin, 'I reckon we better kill off Gineral Sherman first,' and then he laughed and rolled over on the blankets.

"Next mornin' he sent the message, and when the telegraft come back to know if the news was true, he sent word hit was, 'honor bright,' and signed the lieutenant's name, 'James Swann.' Hit was three weeks before the squad got back from Chattanooga way, and all the time Bud kept sendin' lies about great Confederate victories. He was keerful what he sent, too, and figgered on the dates, and kept all the messages he had sent before wrote down in order, so he would n't get mixed. When we got all ready to leave Bear Clift, which was the tenth station, Bud flagged an order to hold on — that relief was comin'.

"Now, after we started east, we picked up a station every mornin'; and as soon as Bud got his hands on the flags, he begun to lie more than ever, closin' up the war with a dash. We had over fifty prisoners when we took the three men off from Upper Bald, and there havin' been six on every other station, we nat'rally thought we had found the last; and the cavalry went away with their prisoners to Quallatown."

CHAPTER XXV

CONCLUSION

AFTER the straightforward story of Tom Zachary, which explained the cunning method by which Lieutenant Coleman and his comrades had been deceived by the flag-messages, the soldiers could feel no resentment toward Tom. They were so happy in the possession of all the good news they had heard that they would have shaken hands with Bud Bryson himself, if he had been one of their rescuers.

"Now I reckon," said the rosy-faced man, as he got on his feet to go down the mountain, "considerin' the way things has turned out, you-all won't keer about investin' in property in this upper kentry, and I'll give ye back your money," he continued, looking fondly at the two yellow coins.

Coleman and Bromley, however, insisted that a bargain was a bargain, and that they wanted the land more than ever. They should go away, they said, the next day if Philip was able to make the journey; and Lieutenant Coleman pressed another coin upon Hooper, for which he was to bring them a supply of clothing which they could wear as far as Asheville.

It all seemed like a dream to the three belated soldiers when their visitors had gone; but Bromley, who was the more practical, reminded his comrades that the antislavery societies must have been long since disbanded, and that the gold was theirs by the right of discovery. So, after making a supper of the corn-bread from the haversack, Coleman and Bromley fell to work with a will, stripping the mill of its golden bands and hinges and hasps; and late into the night the windows of the forge glowed and beamed, and the ruddy firelight streamed out through the cracks in the logs, where Bromley, the goldsmith, was smelting and hammering the precious metal into bars, and beating into each, while it was soft, the impress of a double-eagle, reversed.

When all the gold was packed in the very cask in which they had found it, and so wedged and padded with leaves of the temperance books that it no longer chinked when it was moved, a book-cover was nailed on the head, and the package was addressed to "LIEUTENANT FREDERICK HENRY COLEMAN, U. S. A., WASHINGTON, D. C."

The tin box containing the diary, and the flags and swords and such books as they wished to keep, were gathered together and packed for transportation.

By noon of the following day the two mountaineers appeared again, looking like old-clothes men as they came over the hill.

When the three soldiers got out of their tattered cloth-

"THEY LOOKED HARDLY LESS COMICAL THAN BEFORE."

ing, and into the butternut-and-gray suits which had been borrowed for them from the neighbor folk in the settlement, the misfits were such that they looked hardly less comical than before. Philip was the first to appear from the house ready for the descent. His hat was a bell-crowned beaver, his trousers were turned up half-way to his knees, and he carried in his hand the alligator-skin bag which had belonged to the beautiful lady of the balloon.

After they got down the ladders, Coleman carried the cask as far as the gorge, resting at intervals, but never permitting the two mountaineers to test its weight or even suspect its contents. Philip and Bromley divided between them the flags and sabers, the remaining carbine, the map, and the tin box containing the diary. Hooper and Zachary were occupied with the six sad roosters, and Tumbler, the bear, ambled along behind the men as they picked their way down the mountain. It was really a perilous journey along the rough trunk of the great pine which lay across the dark chasm, but Bromley shouldered the cask, and walked over as steadily as old Tumbler himself, and, arrived on the opposite side, he set it on end in the tail of the steer-cart, which was hitched to a sapling alongside the very rock on which Andy, the guide, had been seated when he told the story of the old man of the mountain.

The tall pines were whispering together in the soft wind as unconcernedly as if it had been seven days instead of seven years since the soldiers had stood on that spot before, and the tinkling stream below was still chinking on its way like silver coins in a vault.

At first Philip mounted the seat beside Tom Zachary, and took charge of the fowls jolting in a yellow, croaking mass between his feet, except the old paralyzed rooster, which he carried tenderly in his lap. He was too excited to ride, however, and presently he got down and walked with the others. At every stage of the descent the soldiers were learning new facts about the war, which made their return to the United States a triumphal and delirious progress. By the time they reached the hill-pastures, where they were greeted by some of the very same copper bells that had startled the cavalcade going up, they began to be joined by the people who had heard of their discovery. They came in twos, and threes, and whole families, to swell their train, so that when they turned into the sandy road through the valley they were attended by a joyous procession of curious followers, which steadily increased until the cart, with the bear shambling alongside, came to a stand by the woodpile of Elder Long, misnamed Shifless. Philip took off his bell-crowned hat right and left to the women; and Lieutenant Coleman greeted Aunt Lucy, who leaned on her crutches at the gate among the purple cabbage-heads, with the stately courtesy he had learned at West Point.

Riley Hooper mounted the woodpile, and announced, with a merry twinkle in his eye, that he and Tom had captured the "harnts" that had been "doin'" the ghost business so long on old Whiteside; at which Aunt Lucy glared through her spectacles as if the remark were a personal affront to her, and the elder exclaimed fervently, "May the Lord's will be done!"

When presently the mail-carrier came along in his one-horse gig, Lieutenant Coleman wrote a hurried despatch to the adjutant-general of the army, announcing the relief of his station, and the cask containing the treasure was committed to the carrier's charge, to be sent on by express, as if it were only the commonest piece of luggage.

When the sun disappeared behind the mountain, ushering in the long twilight in the valley, the crowd was still increasing, and one of the last to arrive was the old postmaster from the Cove. When he came the soldiers and their deliverers were seated with the elder's family about the supper-table in the kitchen, where the neighbors lined the walls and filled the doors and windows, eager to hear more of the life on the mountain.

The great round table itself excited the soldiers' surprise; for, besides being covered with a gaudy patchwork of oilcloth, it was encircled at a lower level with a narrow ledge which held the plates and cups and knives and forks, while the great center was loaded with smoking loaves of corn-bread, platters of fried chicken, bowls of potatoes, jugs of milk, and pots of fragrant tea.

Room was made for the postmaster at the hospitable board, and after the elder had said grace standing, he invited everybody to help himself, at the same time giving the table a twirl which sent the smoking dishes and the flaring tallow dips circling around on an inner clockwork of creaking wooden wheels. It was altogether such a bewildering and unexpected movement that Philip nearly fell out of his chair, and even Bromley, who had just laid a piece of corn-bread on the edge of the oilcloth, dropped his knife as he saw the bread sail around until it rested in front of the postmaster, very much as the blanket had fluttered down from the balloon.

After the supper was over, and all the neighbor folks had been satisfied, eating and drinking where they stood, Lieutenant Coleman, speaking for his companions, related such incidents in connection with their life on the mountain as he chose to disclose. He ended his long story by presenting the bear to Riley Hooper, and the six sad roosters to Tom Zachary, with a sum of money to pay for their keeping. The library of abolition books he presented to Elder Long, telling him where he would find it in the long cavern.

"Hit 's plumb quare," said the postmaster, after Lieutenant Coleman sat down. "Did you 'ns ever drop sech a thing as a spy-glass?"

"We did indeed," said all three of the soldiers together.

"An' mighty well battered an' twisted hit was," said the postmaster. "I found hit 'mongst the rocks a spell after the blanket landed front o' my door, an' I always 'lowed hit fell out o' the balloon."

The soldiers laughed.

"I come dreffful nigh comin' up thar in '69," said the postmaster. "Say, strangers," he continued, dropping his voice, "tell me true; did you 'ns ever view the harnt up yonder?"

"We never had the pleasure," said Lieutenant Coleman.

"That's quare, too," said the postmaster, "an' you livin' thar seven year; fur I viewed hit, an' no mistake, that winter afore I 'lowed to come up, a-gyratin' an' cavortin' on the avalanche in the moonlight, the same bein' the night afore hit fell."

Bromley sat back in his chair, and laughed aloud. "Here's the 'harnt' you saw," he exclaimed, slapping Philip on the shoulders.

"No, no!" cried the postmaster, getting onto his feet with a scared look in his face. "Yer funnin' with me, stranger, fur no human could 'a' got thar whar I viewed the harnt."

"But he did," said Bromley; and then he described how Philip fell, and how he got up again. "By the way," continued Bromley, looking around, "is the young woman present who used to live alone in the house under Sheep Cliff?"

At this question some of the neighbor women pushed forward a tall, stoop-shouldered girl with a sallow face, who struggled to avoid the gaze of the soldiers.

"What fur ye want 'o know?" she said in a sullen voice, still pushing to get back to her place against the wall.

"Oh, nothing," said Philip; "only we used to see you through the telescope."

The soldiers and the family sat for a time in silence after the most of the neighbors had gone.

"Well, I declare," said the postmaster, giving a twirl to the creaking table which caused the last guttering candle to approach him in a smoky circle, "how things do come round!"

The light reddened the postmaster's face for an instant, and gleamed on his glasses, as he blew out the candle and pinched the wick.

And so ends the history of the three soldiers who remained in voluntary exile for seven years, and were happily rescued at last.

www.ingramcontent.com/pod-product-compliance
Lightning Source LLC
Chambersburg PA
CBHW021158230426
43667CB00006B/457